ephen Armstrong is a journalist. He writes for the *Sunday*
nes, *Guardian*, *Esquire, Elle,* Radio 4 and the *New Statesman*
iong others. His first book, *The White Island*, was published
2005 and his second, *War plc: The Rise of the New Corporate*
rcenary, was published in 2008.

THE
SUPER-RICH
SHALL
INHERIT
THE EARTH

STEPHEN ARMSTRONG

Constable • London

Constable & Robinson Ltd
3 The Lanchesters
162 Fulham Palace Road
London W6 9ER
www.constablerobinson.com

First published in the UK by Constable,
an imprint of Constable & Robinson Ltd, 2010

A copy of the British Library Cataloguing in
Publication data is available from the British Library

ISBN: 978-1-84901-041-2

Printed and bound in the EU

1 3 5 7 9 10 8 6 4 2

For Mum, Dad and Matt

CONTENTS

ACKNOWLEDGEMENTS

The existence of this book is entirely down to Rob Blackhurst, who suggested the original idea and introduced me to Becky Hardie at Constable & Robinson – who proved the perfect, tolerant, supportive editor when she had a lot else on her plate. Jaqueline Mitchell copy edited with immense patience.

A number of people's advice helped shape the result, including the mighty Matthew Lynn at Bloomberg, Robert Kelsey at Moorgate Group, Emily L. Walker – formerly of Citigroup, Charles Clover, the *Financial Times*' Moscow correspondent and Johnna Montgomerie at the Economic and Social Research Council's Centre for Research on Socio-Cultural Change.

Grateful thanks are also due to Ni Bing for advice and translation in Shenzhen, Shanghai and Beijing, Ivan Ude in Shanghai, Rupert Hoogewerf, Elizabeth Wasden and the team at Forbes, Karel Williams at the Economic and Social Research Council's Centre for Research on Socio-Cultural Change, Sally Howard for contacts in Sudbury, India and Brazil, Ana Cecelia Martins and Silvio Essinger in São Paulo, Sunita Dubey at Global Action on ArcelorMittal, Bobby Peek at groundWork in South Africa, Daniel Pentzlin at Friends of the Earth Europe, Liam Bailey at Knight Frank estate agents, Margaret Johnson at Leagas Delaney, Nityanand Jayaraman in Chennai, Madhu Dutta in Orissa, Jamil Anderlini in Beijing, Martin Quinn in

Moscow, Rachel Morarjee who knows China, Russia and Szechuan food better than anyone, David Hoffman, Simon Kirby in Shanghai, Kim Zigfeld, David Fleischer at Brazil Focus, the team at *Brazzil* magazine, Mitchel Abolafia at the Rockefeller College of Public Affairs & Policy, Philip Augur, John Plender, Xu Chog Guang in Shenzhen, Yuval Millo and Dr Ruth Katamari at the London School of Economics, Assaf Cohen at 1st Class Security, Frederico do Valle at CapGemini and Greg Baiden in Sudbury. Needless to say, mistakes, inaccuracies and selective editing are mine and mine alone.

I was lucky to have editors commission features that helped in researching this book – notably Richard Cook at *Wallpaper*, Mat Smith at *Esquire* and Paul Clements at the *Daily Telegraph*. Other editors – especially Helen Hawkins at the *Sunday Times*, Jane Martinson at the *Guardian* and Claire Sacre at *Elle* – have been unusually generous throughout. Thanks are also due to Undaleeb Qazi, Britta Jaschinski, Ali Gunning, Hannah and Anna at *HBO*, Will Hodgkinson, Tyler Brulee and Alkarim Jivani.

Nothing would get done without my excellent agent Cat Ledger, who always knows what's what, and everything would be worthless without Rosa, Tess and Georgia.

And finally – novelists always get to quote from poems or songs at the start of their books so I don't see why I shouldn't at the start of a work of non-fiction:

> The battle is getting harder
> In this iration, armagideon time.
> The Clash, 1979

PROLOGUE

IN WHICH AN OLD MAN FIGHTS
A BILLIONAIRE

Strike Matsepo is no Erin Brockovich and yet, in a way, he's a thousand times braver. His corporate enemy towers so high above him that its shadow falls on his tiny house, and though he's been fighting that giant for years, you can see how many blows he's taken. Strike is 80 years old with flecks of grey in his hair and a short, neat beard, lines etched deep into his skin and a wary look in his tired eyes when he first meets you. After a few seconds of conversation, however, he breaks into a warm and welcoming grin and shows you around the rows of vegetables, the squat six-roomed house and the dusty outbuildings that make up his cherished smallholding.

As he leads you – slowly, with shaking legs – through the kitchen and the hall, you can't help but notice how clean every surface is. The bare rooms are sparsely furnished, with angular 1970s furniture resting on dust-free rugs and well-swept floors. Strike is house proud in a way that's hard to understand completely if you haven't been forcefully denied the right to buy your own home. For the first 65 years of his life, Strike lived under apartheid rule in South Africa – a system which banned him from owning property simply because he was black.

He was born in the Orange Free State – the flat boundless plains in the heart of South Africa – where his parents were farm tenants, working for a white landlord but renting land to grow a little of their own produce. Strike didn't go to school – he spent most of his childhood looking after the farmer's cattle. When a foreman from a steel plant in neighbouring Transvaal came recruiting, Strike signed up to be a carpenter and moved north, to the highly industrialized Vanderbjlpark. After ten years and a couple of jobs he ended up as a welder and mechanic at the Coca Cola factory where he stayed for 25 years building up a respectable pension until, in 1990, with South Africa stumbling towards democracy, the laws were changed and anyone could own a house if they wanted.

'This was at the time of Mandela, when people could move where they liked and buy what they liked,' he recalls. 'I wanted to buy a small farm – to keep some pigs and some cattle, to grow some vegetables. So I found this place,' he sweeps his arm across his land – roughly the size of three football pitches. 'It used to be a good place. My children, my sister and my brother – with their children – came to live here. Maybe six children?' he puzzles for a second, then his daughter bustles across the sun-drenched yard and starts counting for him. 'Ten children,' he laughs and points to a brick outhouse. 'The children all had to live there, a hostel,' he jokes, using the word for the workers' hostels often attached to factories in South Africa, where employees sleep in bunk-filled dormitories. 'We would finish a big sack of mealie meal in two weeks.'

But slowly, things started to go wrong. The vegetables grew, but they grew very small. Some of his animals started giving birth to severely damaged young, with hooves stuck together or feet missing entirely. 'One pig was born with his penis in his anus,' Strike gives a brief, wry grin at the dangerous absurdity. He lost some fully grown animals – they shrivelled and died. Once he went to sleep with six cows outside his window and when he woke in the morning they were all dead.

Then his sister got sick. There was blood in her urine and she was very tired all the time. The hospital said she had kidney problems, that it might be cancer, and they started to treat her but, in July 2004, she died. The immediate cause was kidney failure and cancer but the doctors noticed something odd about her blood – very, very high levels of cadmium. The sort of levels that used to be found in workers in badly run industrial plants in the 1950s and 1960s.

Cadmium is a heavy metal – a particularly toxic one. Aside from being carcinogenic, ingestion of any significant amount causes irreversible damage to the liver and kidneys. The bones become soft, lose density, and become weaker and weaker. This causes sharp pains in the joints and back, and massively increases the risk of fractures. The kidneys stop removing acids from the blood, which causes muscle weakness, arthritis and sometimes a deep coma. Over time, the kidneys can shrink by up to 30 per cent before finally shutting down.

In 1970, the German government investigated the source of cadmium leaching into the Rhine Basin – home to zinc, coal and lead mines, battery plants, pigment and acid manufacturers, power plants and the iron and steel industry. Of the 168 tons (171 tonnes) of cadmium produced in the valley, processes involved in the steel industry – burning coal, coke production and the manufacture of iron and steel – accounted for around 98 tons (100 tonnes).

By coincidence, Strike Matsepo's plot of land is literally across the road from a giant slag heap in the grounds of ArcelorMittal's vast Vanderbjlpark steel factory. Some 130 feet (40 metres) high, the mountain of industrial garbage towers over his tiny farm. You can see yellow bulldozers powering across it all day, kicking up plumes of dust as they shovel mounds of black waste around. When the industrial cleaning company Bauerumweltgruppe, or Bauer Environment Group, treated a similarly sized slag heap at the former Neue Maxhuette steel works in Germany, beside 10 million tons (10.1 milllion tonnes) of slag, oil sludge and filter-dust from flue gas treatment, they found a cocktail of deadly organic compounds, heavy metals and cyanide leaching into the ground-water. When Carin Bosman, formerly a water pollution control officer for the South African government, was overseeing Vanderbjlpark in the mid-1990s, she found tar pits and waste water storage dams carrying carcinogenic organic compounds known as phenols. The dams, built in the 1940s, 1950s and 1960s, were completely unlined, meaning water could simply drain away into the soil.

'There is also a physical effect to the slag heap,' Bosman explains. 'The aquifer – the ground-water, or water table – is very shallow in the Steel Valley. It's only around 6 metres [19 feet 7 inches] beneath the surface. The weight of the dump pushing down on the aquifer displaces the water, raising it even higher – to 1 or 2 metres [3 feet 2 inches to 6 feet 4 inches] beneath the surface. Most of the smallholdings around the factory aren't connected to the municipal water [supply] so they use bore-holes, and septic tanks for sewage. The aquifer rising up meant the natural slow process of the septic tanks did not take place and nitrates entered the bore-hole water. Nitrates can bind in the blood in the place of oxygen, causing methemoglobinemia – lack of oxygen in the blood.'

Around the time his sister fell ill, his brother was also found to have abnormally high levels of lead in his system, and Strike decided to take action. With 15 other smallholders in the Steel Valley area he sued the factory to stop it polluting any further and to gain compensation for current victims of pollution.

He had high hopes of success. For one thing, there was a solid historical record of the plant's polluting activities. Founded in the 1940s by the South African government and run by the state-owned Iron and Steel Industrial Corporation, or ISCOR, the plant had been brutally racist – black workers weren't allowed to have training, housing subsidies or pensions, meaning they laboured in menial and exhausting roles. White workers and local residents, however, had already complained about the pollution.

In 1950, white residents near the plant complained about oil in their maize fields. In 1961 the Department of Water Affairs (DWA) warned ISCOR that it might face legal action for compensation over polluted water from the unlined dams. In 1979 an official from the Soil and Irrigation Research Institute found what he suspected were phenols in one of the dams. In 1983 a bore-hole survey found seepage from ponds on site was polluting the ground-water. In 1984, the Department of Water Affairs complained in a letter to ISCOR that smallholdings in the Steel Valley had become so polluted that the ground-water was 'neither suitable for domestic use nor garden irrigation'. A 1988 report for the DWA by the engineering firm Steffen, Robertson & Kirsten – while admitting surveyors had not been able to examine sufficient bore-holes to be certain, expressed the opinion that the ground-water contained 'a number of harmful organic constituents which can be either carcinogenic or non-carcinogenic'. In 1996 residents reported a black effluent from the plant that smelled of oil and burnt the skin. White precipitate covered gardens and roads. One farm – Rietkuil Farm – closed because plants died and animals fell sick. ISCOR announced it would plant a million trees. All of them died. Another report in 1997 found dense non-aqueous phase liquid in the ground-water – a highly carcinogenic black oily liquid – over 2.7 square miles (7 square kilometres).

And this history produced some results for locals. In 1984 a man called Tromp secured a clean water supply from ISCOR after he complained of pollution in his bore-hole. In 1998 a local resident, Johnny Horne, led an all-white group in a case against ISCOR pushing for damages, the plant to be closed down and the valley cleaned up. They used evidence built up by the local government including an archive of DWA complaints about ISCOR's pollution, letters from ISCOR that seemed to acknowledge this pollution and reports from consultants hired by ISCOR that clearly described the problem. The presiding judge, Judge Cloete, made it clear he was prepared to rule in favour of shutting ISCOR down. The company, now privatized, settled out of court, paying Horne R1 million and the rest of his group a healthy R130,000 (roughly $16,000 at the time), buying up their properties. By 2001, the 500-strong Steel Valley community was down to around 20 smallholdings. ISCOR had bought up the rest of the land and was – without admitting anything – piping clean water to the remaining residents while carefully sealing up their bore-holes.

When Strike and his 15 fellow smallholders launched their court case in 2001, therefore, they had some hope of success. They were using essentially the same evidence as Johnny Horne. The old-fashioned privatized state entity had by then recruited a vibrant London-based steel magnate to help run the company. A 'business assistance agreement' between ISCOR and Lakshmi Mittal provided for Mittal to buy a strategic shareholding in the company for $75 million, have two representatives on ISCOR's board as well as running large chunks of ISCOR's business including procurement, performance, technical support, R&D and marketing.

In 2001, Mittal wasn't the world's eighth richest man – he was only 272nd according to *Forbes*. He didn't yet have his full complement of steel plants in Indonesia, Trinidad, Mexico, Turkey,

Kazakhstan, Germany, Ireland, Romania, Algeria, Bosnia, the Czech Republic, Poland, the US, Canada, Macedonia and more. He was, however, well on his way to becoming the world's largest steel producer – a status he has since achieved – and his business tactics were way ahead of the rest of the industry. With a young, go-ahead, first-world-resident visionary like Mittal in charge, Strike reasoned, the bad old days of apartheid-minded management would finally be over.

In fact, the newly constituted company fought harder than the old-school ISCOR. It obtained a gagging order on the 16 court applicants, banning them from speaking publicly or to the press about the case. It fought each document in turn, disputing that the plant was responsible for the pollution of Steel Valley. In 2003 – just as Mittal made a bid for a controlling stake in ISCOR – the court decided it couldn't make a conclusive ruling and dismissed the case. It awarded costs to Mittal and, in the days following the collapse of the case, all 16 received letters from ISCOR demanding costs in full or – if the money was not forthcoming – the right to buy the applicant's house. It offered around R9,000 each (just over $1,000 at the time) for houses bought less than ten years earlier for R52,000. By the end of the year, all but three had accepted terms and moved away. Strike was holding out for a deal that would at least give him the chance to buy an equal-sized house when his lawyer came up with legal aid to pay the remains of ISCOR's costs. He could stay.

His house and land now stand alone in the middle of a vast barren field where once a large, diverse community with shops and local businesses thrived. Around the edge of his land, ArcelorMittal has erected a high electric fence. Indeed, all the land that once was Steel Valley is fenced off in a similar way. And all that land is now owned by ArcelorMittal. What isn't clear is why. Why would someone buy up an entire town – often against the residents' will – then knock the whole place down, erect massive electric fences around it and abandon it? There are no plans to redevelop the massive space, no plans to farm it, no plans to clean it up. Indeed, at a meeting with ArcelorMittal management in the factory boardroom, I was told 'We have no plans at all for Steel Valley.' There is talk of it acting as a 'green buffer' around the plant, but Steel Valley is only on one side of the factory – the side, as it happens, that is downstream in ground-water terms. The side towards which any pollution reaching the water table would flow.

Strike tried to keep his smallholding productive. He worked the land, raised cattle, looked after his dead sister's children. He became a priest and healer. In the end he gave up keeping livestock for good.

'I feel very sad,' he explains. 'I had hoped to use my pension money to build something that I could give to my children and grandchildren, but now that's all been blown out.' He shakes my hand and goes off to sprinkle water on his wilting lettuce beds, the last smallholder in Steel Valley.

Carin Bosman, who now works for the environmental consultancy Sustainable Solutions, believes the whole area could be rehabilitated. Assuming pollution from the factory is stopped from entering the air and ground-water, there are treatments that could clean out the ground-water and restore the soil. 'They're not cheap,' she says carefully. In fact, the complete rehabilitation of Steel Valley could cost around $60 million. It's an enormous sum of money. And it's roughly the same amount of money Lakshmi Mittal spent on his daughter's wedding in 2004, a few months after his company started purchasing homes at knockdown prices in Steel Valley to cover costs in a court case that had reached no conclusion.

During a meeting at ArcelorMittal with Nku Nyembezi-Heita – the company's CEO – she tried to put a lot of distance between the European ArcelorMittal and the South African company, however. Her ArcelorMittal is a legally constituted South African company. Mittal's shareholding, she insisted, was only 52 per cent. The group offers advice and sets bench-marks but really the local managers manage. Some of her workers disagree, saying production targets change overnight following phone calls from Europe – 'Lakshmi calls Nku and the next day everything changes,' said one union shop steward. Certainly Lakshmi Mittal travels to South Africa regularly. Indeed, he is a member of the presidential advisory committee – a group of ten industrialists who advise the South African president on the country's policy towards corporations. Effectively, he advises South Africa on how to run its economy. Would he really let his own steel mill run itself?

That doesn't sit well with the way Lakshmi Mittal usually operates. The world's eighth richest man is legendarily hands-on. Profiles talk of his talent for spotting under-utilized plants, often in low-cost corners of the world, and making them productive. His empire, employing more than 200,000 people, spans 60 countries and although only 1 per cent of his workforce is based in Britain, he chooses to live there, running his empire from London.

'London is my home now,' he has said. 'It is very convenient. I can fly anywhere at short notice, you are in a much better time zone than the US, and it is a very lovely city. The whole family is here. They all love being in London.'[1] And when it comes to the super-rich, Lakshmi is far from alone. The last ten years have seen billionaires arrive in Britain by the truck-load – or perhaps, by the stretch-limo-load. In part, this is because the country's treatment of wealthy, officially non-domiciled foreigners is very generous. Although there have been a few changes recently, they are broadly still taxed in the normal way on their UK income or money earned from the UK but largely avoid UK taxation on money made overseas. Given most of them make most of their money outside the UK, this means they can stay while paying very little tax indeed while laundering their past and personality so that within a generation they are embedded at the heart of the establishment.

As a result, London can now boast the densest concentration of billionaires on earth. They come from Russia, the Middle East, the US and Asia, they fuelled the recent boom and they are still snapping up homes in Mayfair for millions. Britain not only offers generous tax breaks as well as international political support and lobbying, but even – as in the case of the former Russian spy and dissident Alexander Litvinenko, who was poisoned in London in 2006 – will take up arms on their behalf and pursue those who threaten or harm them around the world.

How did they get here? Essentially they came because the world changed, turning on a handful of political and economic decisions at the end of the 1980s and start of the 1990s. In London in 1986, the Thatcher government deregulated the City in the Big Bang – something Professor Karel Williams at Manchester University's Centre for Research on Socio-Cultural Change describes as 'an anti-democratic coup'. In the same year, Mikhail Gorbachev began loosening the Soviet state's grip on the economy through glasnost. By 1991, post-independence India, constrained by the so-called Licence Raj – the economic system mixing government controls and capitalist trading that was founded by India's first prime minister, Jawaharlal Nehru, was close to collapse and the country was running out of money to buy essentials so it brokered a deal with the International Monetary Fund (IMF) to liberalize its economy. In 1992 Deng Xiaoping, leader of the Chinese Communist Party, announced that China would open itself to foreign investment and abandon theoretical principles of egalitarianism. In the same year, Itamar Franco took over as president of Brazil from his impeached party boss Fernando Collor as inflation reached 1,100 per cent, and launched the Plano Real, stabilizing and modernizing the economy.

In 2001, Jim O'Neill, head of global economic research at Goldman Sachs, produced Global Economics Paper No. 99 – 'Dreaming with BRICs', coining the term to describe the emerging economies of, obviously, Brazil, Russia, India and China. The report predicted growth of 3.6 per cent for Brazil, estimating it would overtake Italy by 2025, France by 2031 and the UK and Germany by 2036. The Goldman Sachs team saw China's growth slipping to 5 per cent by 2020 but still expected it to become the world's largest economy by 2040. India's forecasts were the healthiest of all – growth above 5 per cent through to 2050, outstripping Japan by 2032 while Russia, Goldman Sachs warned, might be hampered by a shrinking population but should still overtake Italy in 2018, France in 2024, the UK in 2027 and Germany in 2029.

Seven years later, the performance of the emerging stock markets was running well ahead of the bank's high expectations. At the end of 2008, even after the year's falls, Brazilian shares were up by 345 per cent since November 2001, India's by 390 per cent, Russia's by 639 per cent and China's, depending on whether you go by the mainland or the Hong Kong exchange, by 26 per cent or 500 per cent. In 2001 Goldman Sachs had predicted that by the end of the decade the BRIC economies would account for 10 per cent of global gross domestic product (GDP) at purchasing power parity (PPP); by 2007 their share was already 14 per cent. The investment bank now expects China's GDP to surpass America's before 2030. Most economists believe that this upward trend will not be seriously broken by the current economic slowdown. Nor is it restricted to the BRICs. In 2005, for the first time since the dawning of the industrial age, emerging economies accounted for more than half of global GDP at PPP.

This should be good news. Increasing wealth should prevent poverty and starvation. Indeed, in April 2007 the World Bank announced that 986 million people worldwide suffered from extreme poverty – the first time its count had dropped below 1 billion. In August 2008, however, it had grim news to report. According to two of its leading researchers, Shaohua Chen and Martin Ravallion, the 'developing world is poorer than we thought'.[2] The correct number was actually almost 1.4 billion. Half of the populations of India and China still relied on wood, charcoal and dung to cook their food.

A little earlier in 2008, the business magazine *Forbes* published its annual list of the world's billionaires and hailed the dawning of a new era. *Forbes* has been producing its global list for 22 years – its debut list in 1986 reported 140 billionaires worldwide. In 2006, half of the world's 20 richest were from the US. In 2008 only four were, while India won bragging rights for its domination of the top ten – four out of ten, more than any other country.

For the first time, in 2008, the number of billionaires *Forbes* could identify crossed into four figures, reaching 1,125. Their total net worth was $4.4 trillion, up $900 billion from the previous year. A third of the new billionaires came from Russia (35), China (28) and India (19). Russia, with a total of 87 billionaires, came in at number two – behind the US and easily overtaking Germany, which had held the honour for six years but whose total of 59 didn't even come close.

Many of these new BRIC billionaires made their money from industries the West was moving away from. The top 20 featured steel tycoon Mittal at number four, India's petrochemical giant Mukesh Ambani at five, his estranged brother Anil at six, Indian real estate baron K.P. Singh at eight, Russian aluminium magnate Oleg Deripaska at nine, Chinese shipping billionaire Li Ka-shing at ten, Russian oil, steel and mining oligarch

Roman Abramovich at 15, his car maker and coal mining compatriot Alexei Mordashov at 18 and Ukrainian oil and banking mogul Mikhail Fridman at 20. They all own industries that will materially affect our lives as the world faces oil, mineral and food depletion in the coming years. They all operate internationally, buying plants, mines and businesses all over the world. Few have shareholders; their companies exist wherever they are and their word is law. We are entering an economic system you could call The New Feudalism.

* * *

This book originally set out simply to explore the increasing power of these developing world super-rich, the effect that would have on our lives and whether we were seeing the arrival of a new non-democratic multi-national super-class. The run on Northern Rock, the failures of Bear Stearns, Lehman Brothers, the Royal Bank of Scotland *et al.* appeared briefly to argue against this thesis. The Russians required government money to totter along; the Indian stock market fell. In March 2009, *Forbes'* annual Rich List estimated that the number of billionaires in the world had fallen by nearly 30 per cent over the previous 12 months. The number of people who could call themselves billionaires in US dollar terms dropped from 1,125 to 793 – the first year since 2003 that the billionaires' club had contracted.

The *Sunday Times* Rich List, published just over a month later, painted a similar picture in the UK. The paper's figures showed the recession wiping £155 billion from the fortunes of Britain's richest 1,000 people, equivalent to more than a third of their wealth and the biggest annual fall since the list began 21 years ago. The number of billionaires in the list fell from 75 to 43. Between them, people ranked in the top 100 lost £92 billion. Only three saw their wealth increase.

In 2009, however, Citibank chief executive Vikram Pandit began work on restructuring the bank, telling senior staff it would effectively become two separate banks, one serving the West – 'massive debt, slow growth' – and the other serving the BRIC countries – 'little debt, massive growth'. Brazil appeared to have skirted the recession entirely while India and China had taken a light hit but seemed back on course. Russia's problems were more complex, but the slump had removed the old animosity between Russian President Putin's reign and the oligarchs – which accounted for many of the permanent London residents from the ranks of Russia's wealthy who had fled his wrath. The story of the slump appeared to be simple – the developing world did better and kept their oligarchs in place while the poor old liberal democracies suffered but remained free.

In May 2009, however, Simon Johnson, Professor of Entrepreneurship at MIT Sloan School of Management and former chief economist at the IMF, realized the slump had uncovered a broader, more menacing trend. Writing in *Atlantic Monthly* in May 2009, Johnson described the US economy thus: 'Just as we have the world's most advanced economy, military, and technology, we also have its most advanced oligarchy.'

Johnson identified a network of cronies, old boys, financiers, politicians and high net worth individuals with a network of connections and patronage that linked Wall Street and Washington more intimately than Putin and his oligarchs. Robert Rubin, once the co-chairman of Goldman Sachs, served in Washington as Treasury Secretary under Clinton, and later became chairman of Citigroup's executive committee. Henry Paulson, CEO of Goldman Sachs during the long boom, became Treasury Secretary under George W. Bush. John Snow, Paulson's predecessor, left to become chairman of Cerberus Capital Management, a large private equity firm that also counts Dan Quayle among its executives. Alan Greenspan, after leaving the Federal Reserve, became a consultant to Pimco, perhaps the biggest player in the international bond markets.

As a result, Johnson argues, 'the oligarchy and the [US] government' had been behaving like an emerging nation with vested and deeply rooted business interests that took no account of the wants or needs of the citizens. In particular, the deals to bail out the financial sector reminded him of Russia in 1998. 'Some of these deals may have been reasonable responses to the immediate situation,' he accepted, writing about America in 2008.

> But it was never clear (and still isn't) what combination of interests was being served, and how. Treasury and the Fed did not act according to any publicly articulated principles, but just worked out a transaction and claimed it was the best that could be done under the circumstances. This was late-night, backroom dealing, pure and simple.[3]

In other words, as far as the man from the IMF was concerned, the recession showed that the financial story of the past ten years wasn't about the hyped-up booms of 1999 and 2007 – now revealed as Ponzi schemes both literally and metaphorically. It was that the rise of the super-rich in the BRIC countries was mirrored by the rise of a similar, unnoticed oligarch class in the West. Others went further.

Around the same time, an article by Bloomberg analyst Matthew Lynn in the *Sunday Times* took a shot at predicting Britain's post-recession economy. 'Capitalism in the post-credit crunch era is going to look much more like the state-dominated, oligarchic but fiercely competitive and dynamic systems of the rising BRIC economies of Brazil, Russia, India and China,' he decided.[4]

When we went for a drink on a slow, sunny afternoon in an old pub near Farringdon station in London, Matthew Lynn unpicked his thinking a little.

> For a decade now we've seen the BRIC companies becoming more and more important but we thought that they'd become like us. We thought they'd go like the Japanese in the 1950s and 1960s and the Koreans in the 1970s and 1980s, emerging in a more or less American/ European-style capitalism. Sony and Toyota pretty much do what we do only slightly better. So we had a basis for thinking China and Brazil, they'll get richer and richer and then they'll do what we do, have a stock market, big corporations, chief executives and have companies like Heinz or Nestlé. We thought they'd end up looking like us, but actually we'll end up looking like them.

The thing about BRIC-style capitalism, he argued, is that it's much harder to understand how things get done. It's like a club and ordinary punters aren't allowed to know the address let alone the membership criteria. In Russia, Dmitry Medvedev goes from running Gazprom to being president. Putin goes from president to prime minister but remains in charge. So what exactly is the relationship between the company and the Russian state?

'If you want to build a tin mine in Russia it's no good just being good at tin mining,' Lynn believes:

> Who cares? Anyone can do that. You've got to know the right person in the Party. Same in China – you have to know the right people, take them out to the right dinners and marry your son to the right daughter – which we don't really do in this country. Here we have – you want to build a

chip factory? What's your business plan? And yet that may not last. We will have a semi-nationalized banking system for quite a long time. If you need access to capital you will need political friends and that might mean making donations or building factories in marginal constituencies. We assumed a necessary condition of wealth and maturity is that you arrive at a liberal capitalism model with companies that operate to a set of ideas and values and are roughly held accountable by society. In fact it may go the other way.

* * *

To an extent we have been here before – in nineteenth-century America with the rule of the Robber Barons. Even if their once mighty empires now look like small fry compared to Abramovich and Mittal, Andrew Carnegie, John D. Rockefeller, Cornelius Vanderbilt, John Jacob Astor and JPMorganChase set the course for today's billionaires. If the Russians engage in dubious share dealings, so did they. If Mittal fights vicious merger battles, so did they. If today's tycoons have an uneasy relationship with government and a terrible relationship with their workforce, so, of course, did they.

They created their wealth through the same swift opportunism, taking advantage of the massive industrialization and rapid technological advances spreading across nineteenth-century America. Half of them made their fortunes in the railways, and the secret of their success was acquiring land from the US government for free – an early version of loans-for-shares and something that was as close to a licence to print money as Russian president Boris Yeltsin's share issue.

These days Carnegie, Morgan, Rockefeller and Vanderbilt are familiar names even to those who care little about economic history. Vanderbilt started out as a poor Staten Island farmer

boy, then built an enormous fortune in steamships and rail-
roading. Rockefeller, the son of a travelling salesman, forged
his mighty Standard Oil by undercutting rivals thanks to secret
rebates from the railroads bringing oil into his home state of
Cleveland. They lived in, and arguably created, the period in
US history dubbed the Gilded Age by Mark Twain.

Having amassed huge personal fortunes, these billionaires
certainly engaged in extensive philanthropy, but they weren't
exactly giving all their money away. Carnegie built Dungeness,
a 59-room Queen Anne-style mansion, on Cumberland Island,
just off the coast of Georgia. Morgan owned several yachts
and, legend has it, when asked about the cost of maintaining
them replied, 'If you have to ask the price, you can't afford it.'
Vanderbilt preferred to splurge money on racehorses.

Their unethical and often illegal business practices so
incensed the US journalist and historian Matthew Josephson
that he dubbed them the Robber Barons after a group of feudal
lords who charged exorbitant tolls to ships sailing up and down
the Rhine, using soldiers, steel chains and castles to enforce
their monopolies. His 1934 book, called simply *Robber Barons*,
outlined their history thus:

> The barons had such great panache with their private palace
> cars on rails, their imitation Renaissance castles and their
> pleasure yachts – one of which JPMorgan defiantly chris-
> tened the *Corsair*. The expanding America of the post-Civil
> War era was the paradise of [these] freebooting capitalists
> – untrammeled and untaxed. They demanded always a free
> hand in the market, promising that in enriching themselves
> they would 'build up the country' for the benefit of all the
> people. The Americans of those days had no time for the arts
> of civilization but turned as with a single impulse to the
> huge tasks of developing their continent . . . All of this was

achieved in a climactic quarter-century . . . with much haste, much public scandal and without plan under the leadership of a small class of parvenus. Theirs is a story of a well-nigh irresistible drive toward monopoly, which the plain citizens, Congress and presidents opposed – seemingly in vain.

Only three times over the twentieth century has 5 per cent of America's national income gone to families in the richest one-hundredth of a per cent, according to the economists Emmanuel Saez at the University of California, Berkeley and Thomas Piketty at the Paris School of Economics: in 1915 and 1916, as the Gilded Age was ending; briefly in the late 1920s, before the stock-market crash; and most recently at the beginning of the twenty-first century.

In the first two cases, such over-centralized wealth and power caused governments to act. The Robber Barons' empires were broken up by the Sherman Antitrust Act, which was passed in 1890 but found its form at the beginning of the twentieth century. By 1900, for instance, John D. Rockefeller's Standard Oil controlled over 90 per cent of the refined oil in the United States, could set prices to maximize profits and could bludgeon suppliers into cutting costs. On 15 May 1911 Rockefeller was on the golf course when he was told that the Supreme Court had found the firm guilty of anti-trust violations and had ordered it to be broken up. So vast was Standard Oil's monopoly that the resulting 34 companies included giants like Exxon, Amoco, Mobil and Chevron.

The Act remains on the statute books in the US, just as anti-monopoly legislation exists in most Western countries. These should be bulwarks against the excessive power of the super-rich should they attempt price-fixing or cartel-style behaviour – which critics say they already are. In September 2009, for instance, ArcelorMittal in South Africa and two other steel producers were accused of 'cartel activity, which involved price-fixing' by South Africa's Competition Commission – which said it would seek huge fines of as much as 10 per cent of revenue, as the price-fixing came at a time when South Africa was spending R787 billion ($102 billion) over three years on power, rail and road projects preparing to host 2010's World Cup.

What's different today, however, is the international nature of this oligarchy. As the furore over the non-domicile tax rate has shown, many of these individuals have no concern for the nation state – they can simply move to another of their houses in some other country or some other continent and carry on business as usual.

According to Frederico do Valle, lead consultant in wealth management at Capgemini Financial Services:

> Ultra high net worth individuals – people with $30 million or more in investable assets – are becoming more globe trotting due to the regulatory environment and now that's impacting their view of where they live. They don't want to commit to one nation. We have a client who lives on his boat and he just moves around because he doesn't want to be stuck in one tax jurisdiction permanently.

Yet, instead of passing laws restricting the super-rich – as with the Sherman Act – national governments have ignored, supported or actively rescued these vast multinational monopolies, with their wealth still unscrutinized and unassailable. And the threat is greater: in 1890 peak oil was inconceivable. Now we're conscious that oil and mineral wealth is finite. The scramble to impress rather than regulate shows that few nation states tower above the super-rich in terms of the power they can exert. Bill Gates's personal wealth outstrips the GDP of Lithuania, Sri Lanka and Kenya; Lakshmi Mittal is ahead of Jordan and

Cameroon; while Chinese billionaire Li Ka-shing tops Zambia, Jamaica and Uganda.

Even non-governmental organizations (NGOs) like Global Action on ArcelorMittal – a coalition of community and environmental groups from around the world working to get ArcelorMittal to invest in pollution prevention and health and safety at its steel mills and coal and iron ore mines – is worried that the company's response might be to just up and leave troublesome countries.

'The problem with these huge personally run companies is that they are stronger than any one country,' the NGO's co-ordinator Sunita Dubey explains. 'That's how Lakshmi Mittal secures loans from public banks and huge favours from governments.'

And their power over those governments is not just the threat of unemployment. 'The weaponization of Russia's oil revenues poses the most serious threat to Western security, especially since [the companies of] many oligarchs are used as fronts to conceal the Kremlin's actions,' according to Kim Zigfeld, a New York City-based writer who publishes her own Russia speciality blog and writes about the country for US media out- lets. She continues:

> Obviously, Russia's ability to threaten economic warfare depends almost entirely on the price of oil, but we should not be entirely sanguine when we see that price fall. It backs Russia into a corner, inducing it to begin to play nasty hardball in the style of the old USSR. I see the recent gas cut-offs in Ukraine not as an attack on Ukraine itself, though Russia doubtless has designs on it just as it has on Georgia, but as an effort to destabilize markets and squeeze more money out of Europe. Russia has the same interest in destabilizing the Middle East, to drive up the price of oil,

and its action in Georgia indicates clearly the lengths it is prepared to go to in order to vent its spleen.

Zigfeld is referring to the disputes, in March 2005, over prices paid by Russia to send its gas to Europe through the Ukraine's pipeline system which led to Putin's government cutting off all gas supplies to Ukraine on 1 January 2006. Eventually, four days later, the supply was restored, and an agreement hashed out between the countries.

A second dispute in October 2007 over gas debts led to a reduction in gas supplies and, during the last months of 2008, fresh tension led to 18 European countries reporting major falls or cut-offs in their gas supplies from Russia. In a bid to stabilize the situation, the IMF, the World Bank and the European Bank for Reconstruction and Development (EBRD) agreed a loan of $1.7 billion to help the Ukraine provide stable supplies of gas to Europe.

In 2009, Britain's energy demand hit 59 gigawatts – over 45 per cent of which was supplied from North Sea gas with 35 per cent from coal, 15 per cent from nuclear energy and the rest from a variety of sources. Assuming modest economic growth, *The Economist* estimates the country will need around 64 gigawatts to cope with peak conditions by 2015. Meeting that demand could be a problem.

North Sea gas has served Britain well over the years but its supply peaked in 1999. Since then the flow has halved. By 2015 it will have dropped a further two-thirds. By 2015, four of Britain's ten nuclear power stations will have shut and no new ones will be ready for years. As for coal, Britain will be breaking just about every green promise it has ever made if it is using anything like as much as it does today. Renewable energy sources will help, but these can be on-off forces and won't easily replace more predictable gas, nuclear and coal power in their current technological form. There will be a shortfall – perhaps of as much as 20 gigawatts. This will, most likely, be met by imported gas – the largest and easiest supplier of which is Russia.

Lord Cameron of Dillington, a farmer and the first head of the Countryside Agency, was commissioned to explore the effects of an all-out four-day oil embargo as experienced by Ukraine in 2006. His scenario imagined a sudden shut-down, so that petrol already in the system was all that was left. By the end of day one, he predicted, there would be panic buying and stocking up of shelves – thus emptying supermarkets quicker than the fleet of lorries, with their dwindling fuel supplies, could replenish them. By the end of day two, shops would be almost empty, and by day three – well, Lord Cameron coined the phrase 'nine meals from anarchy'.[5]

If the UK turns away from an oil-based economy to avoid this peril, how will it generate the power it needs? Hybrid cars and wind turbines may offer some hope, and yet both these technologies require an unusual metal known as a rare earth element. Of this, 99 per cent of the planet's supply is in China – some 50 per cent of the mines in state hands and 50 per cent run by so-called 'red hat' capitalists. The country has been reducing export quotas of rare earth elements over the past three years with plans for further restrictions to ensure greater profits from its monopoly. Britain's green alternative is in China's hands.

In 2000, Naomi Klein's *No Logo* described a vision for the decade of rapacious corporations building brands at the expense of impoverished Third World employees and ripped-off First World consumers. In kneeling before the Golden Arches of McDonald's or the mighty Swoosh of Nike, we were being sold a pup. The time had come, Naomi Klein argued, to protest – and protest we did. Corporations adopted socially concerned policies, high street fashion chain Zara ended its contracts with a supplier that worked with factories employing sweat-shop labour and Starbucks started selling Fair Trade coffee. Even McDonald's has moved to meet the outrage – becoming, in 2009, the UK's third largest buyer of organic milk. Only eight years later *No Logo* looks almost optimistic. If you want to protest about oligarch behaviour, first find them, then try and wave a banner. Most have small private armies, bullet-proof cars, armoured yachts and no intention of losing a cent.

*   *   *

This book tries to understand our new oligarch planet. It looks at the rise of the developing world oligarchs and the lives they lead, at the dubious means by which most of them achieved their wealth and political influence and it plots how the West has produced its own cronyistic and anti-democratic oligarchy. It argues that we face a great threat to our freedom and to our democratic rights and that we have to take action – but that street protests and shareholder meetings are rapidly losing their power against these back-room billionaires and their friends in government.

Although I approached most of the super-rich named in this book for interview, none granted that request. Many of my actual interviewees asked for anonymity and I have respected that. I'm a journalist, not an academic, so interviews conducted between October 2008 and November 2009 make up the vast majority of this book, whether quoted directly or used as sources of information. Sometimes I've used and referred to books, newspapers, broadcasts and research papers. Parts of the book, necessarily, try to sum up huge and complex moments in social and economic history a little too briefly, but there's a list of suggested books for further reading where readers may expand on these truncated accounts. Where possible, I've tried to look at the events described through the eyes of those involved.

In telling the stories of the super-rich, it makes sense to start with Russia. It is the best-known oligarch home and its recent history sets the scene with startling clarity. As the Soviet Union collapsed, an entrepreneurial group of social outsiders lobbied and bribed officials for government contracts, tax exemptions, subsidies and protection from foreign competitors. State hand-outs were their beachhead. Wealth accumulation resulted from the sell-off of banks, minerals, energy resources, telecommunications, power plants and transport and the assumption by the state of private debt. The billionaires consolidated and expanded through mergers, acquisitions, further privatizations and overseas expansion. Relationships between government and the super-rich were alternately cosy and perilous. This pattern holds largely true for all four of the BRIC developing countries and these entrepreneurial outsiders could come from São Paulo, Shanghai or New Delhi – but we will begin with Moscow.

CHAPTER ONE

IN WHICH BORIS FINDS A
MONEY SPIDER

Alexander Litvinenko's funeral took place on a bleak, rain-soaked afternoon in December. After a short service at Regent's Park mosque, his wife and 12-year-old son led some 50 mourners through the puddles of a tree-lined avenue in Highgate Cemetery – it is unoriginal but irresistible to point out that Highgate also contains Karl Marx's grave.

Boris Berezovksy, the super-rich Russian industrialist and media magnate, and Chechen separatist leader Akhmed Zakayev were among the many grim-faced pallbearers – a gang of men huddled together to lift his coffin rather than the traditional stately six. Litvinenko's coffin was heavy-duty oak, with air-tight seals and a lead lining to prevent radiation seeping from his raddled corpse.

The two men had persuaded Litvinenko to join them in London when they fled Putin's wrath. A former spy who had become a fierce critic of the Russian government, Litvinenko had been a vital part of their PR campaign, claiming he had information that Putin had plotted to murder Berezovsky and had conspired to blame Zakayev for attacks on Moscow apartment blocks by the Federal Security Service (FSB) – the renamed KGB. His accusations helped persuade British courts not to grant Russia's extradition requests for both men.

Perhaps it was this testimony that led to his murder – conspiracy theories abound. The basic facts are complicated enough and make ideal fodder for the paranoid. On 1 November 2006, Litvinenko had met former KGB men Andrei Lugovoi and Dimitri Kovtun in the Pine Bar at London's Millennium Mayfair hotel, then had lunch with Italian academic Mario Scaramella at Itsu sushi bar. Several hours later he had complained of feeling sick and spent the night vomiting, ultimately being admitted to University College Hospital where he had died on 23 November from polonium poisoning. He had issued a statement on his deathbed accusing Putin of ordering his death.

As his body was lowered into the ground, Russian authorities slapped restrictions on the nine Metropolitan Police detectives who had travelled to Moscow to investigate his murder. The Met refused to be cowed and every detail of the investigation that followed was impressive. In May 2007, after a number of police trips as well as extensive searches of hotel rooms, bars, restaurants and aeroplanes, the Director of Public Prosecutions recommended Lugovoi should be charged with Litvinenko's murder. Russia refused extradition requests and the resulting diplomatic wrangle saw tit-for-tat expulsions of diplomats and a decline in relations between the two countries.

And while Litvinenko, as a critic and ex-spy, had specific reasons for seeking safe refuge in the UK, he was not the only one to fear Putin's far-ranging powers. When Putin became president in 2000, many oligarchs also feared for their wealth and safety. A long-term employee of London's famous Roman

Abramovich voices a widely held belief, for instance, that 'the reason Roman bought Chelsea was to protect himself from assassination'.

The press and public largely approved of the Met's actions in the Litvinenko case, and have broadly welcomed these wealthy outsiders. After all, what's not to like? Russian oligarchs look like so much fun. They bring wealth, glamour and the prospect of international success for previously mediocre Premier League teams.

Take Abramovich. His lifestyle spending alone reads like the state acquisitions of a moderately ambitious nation. In 2008 he bought Francis Bacon's *Triptych* for $86.3 million at Sotheby's New York, as well as splashing out $33.6 million on Lucian Freud's *Benefits Supervisor Sleeping* at Christie's. Both sales made history in the art world. Abramovich's bid for Bacon's *Triptych* was the highest price yet paid for a post-war work of art while Freud became the world's most expensive living artist at auction.

The tycoon owned a country estate in West Sussex, which he bought in 1999 for £12 million from the Australian media magnate Kerry Packer (since given to his wife as part of a divorce settlement). The 420-acre (170-hectare) estate at Fyning Hill near Rogate boasts a seven-bedroom house, an indoor pool and jacuzzi with plunge pool, two polo pitches, stables for 100 horses, a tennis court, a rifle range, a trout lake and even a go-kart track. Media reports claim he ordered 20,000 grouse and pheasants so he could enjoy a spot of shooting.

In 2004, he bought a 12-bedroom villa on the French Riviera at Cap d'Antibes between Nice and Cannes. Built for an English aristocrat in Victorian style in 1927, Château de la Croë was once the residence of the Duke and Duchess of Windsor. Previous owners include the Belgian King Leopold II, Aristotle Onassis and Greta Garbo.

In 2008 he bought Wildcat Ridge, a mansion near Aspen, Colorado, from Leon Hirsch, former head of the medical firm US Surgical, for $36 million and, at the same time, began plans to build the most expensive private residence in Britain – a £150 million mansion in Knightsbridge spread across two stucco-fronted properties running over eight floors in Lowndes Square. In 2009 he splashed out £55 million on a 70-acre (28-hectare) estate on the Caribbean island of St Barthélemy. The charming little retreat looks out on to Gouverneur Bay, where the oligarch will be able to moor his new yacht and flagship of 'Abramovich's navy' – the *Eclipse*.

This boat, launched in the summer of 2009, cost £724 million. It boasts two helipads, two swimming pools – the larger of which doubles up as a dance floor when drained – and 6 foot-wide (1.8 metres-wide) home cinema screens in all 24 guest cabins. The master suite has a retractable roof so that Roman and his girlfriend Daria Zukhova can sunbathe or sleep beneath the stars. The hull and windows are strong enough to withstand a direct missile attack and the yacht has a French-built missile defence system fitted aboard. In case of less sophisticated assaults, the crew of 60 includes a security team of French Foreign Legion veterans and there's also an anti-paparazzi laser shield. If infra-red lasers detect electronic light sensors in a nearby camera the system fires a focused beam of light at the lens, disrupting its picture.

The *Eclipse* joins Roman's super-yacht, the 377-foot (115-metre) £100 million *Pelorus* – which has only one helipad but does offer a cinema – as well as the yachts *Sussurro* and *Ecstasea*. Abramovich also owns two submarines. His first, a 118-foot (36-metre) Seattle 1000, commissioned from the leading manufacturer US Submarines, cost £13 million to buy and takes a further £1 million a year to run. With two deck levels, separate living areas for guests and crew, dining-rooms and state-rooms, the boat is capable of diving to a depth of 1,000 feet (305 metres) and can remain submerged for two weeks. He is said to have a second sub on order from US Submarines, a smaller 65-foot (20-metre) Nomad 1000, which cost £3 million and will dock on the *Eclipse*.

On land, Abramovich owns a number of cars, including a £1 million Ferrari FXX racing car. In the air he has a Boeing 767, known as 'The Bandit'. Originally designed to seat 360 people, it has been refitted with a two-level bedroom, a lounge, offices, a kitchen and a crew area. Like the *Eclipse*, it also features a sophisticated anti-missile system – which suggests a certain level of paranoia.

The aeroplane was famously used to pick up sushi from London when Roman was on an overseas work trip. On another occasion, according to one Condé Nast staffer, when Abramovich's girlfriend Dasha, the editor of style magazine *Pop*, was told 'it was impossible to use the paper she wanted because it was only available in Germany and they didn't have time to ship it over, she replied, "Well, I have a plane."'

Roman's toys are by no means unique. 'Today, a megayacht is indispensable,' argues Olivier Milliex, head of yacht finance at the Dutch bank ING. 'It's not like ten years ago when a yacht was a luxury item and 100 metres [328 feet] was thought big. Yacht sales have increased 10–15 per cent in the last few years and now everyone's shopping for mini-submarines and heli-copters to go with their new purchase.'

According to Luca Bassani, founder and CEO of Wally Yachts, all boat interiors were essentially identical ten years ago. 'You had one or two cockpits, one or two cabins, the galley and the crew rooms. They were all done in the same style – shag carpet and lots of wood – whether they were motor or sail.' The new rich, Bassani says, want gyms, spas, cinemas and recording studios and they want them styled with bespoke interiors. 'You might have eternity pools with waterfalls going down to the smaller pool on the deck below,' he explains. 'Interiors are polycentric – haptic surfaces that you can see, touch and feel for different sensations. There's a love of carbon fibre and Macassar Ebony – because these people are rich and they want the best and they want it as soon as possible.'

Bassani's experience chimes with designers in the private jet and high-end interiors world. As the super-rich started spending on their homes and playthings, they found an annoying little trend that quite put them off their quail's egg soufflé. In the early 1990s, style was a preserve of the precious few – if you owned a Barber Osgerby Loop Coffee Table or the Jasper Morrison Cappellini Low Pad Chair you could rest your feet on them safe in the knowledge that they would elicit gasps of awe from the right sort of person as they plucked their California roll with Hermès chop-sticks. Over the last decade, however, makeover TV programmes and high street home furnishing shops have offered almost everyone the chance to acquire cheap imitations for a fraction of the cost. The basic problem for luxury design was this: if McDonald's is using modernist furniture in its burger bars, what does the top end use to demonstrate their wealth?

Paul Davies is a developer and interior designer who specializes in property in New York, Monaco and London, with the 'golden triangle' of Belgravia, Knightsbridge and Mayfair providing the greatest growth. His clients are 'wealthy international people in their forties or fifties who live in a number of different places at a time', he explains. 'They've made their money in oil, manufacturing and shipping, with a few in hedge funds, and they'll have four or five homes – one where they're from, somewhere in the US, London, and a holiday home on an island.'

His clients want an overall design package that unites each house but with specific local differences. 'Homes used to be a catalogue of a person's life,' he explains. 'Today the wives of the mega-rich have no wish to decorate and furnish. Now, homes are all about having different looks for when people are in different parts of the world for different reasons. People don't have the inclination to decorate or design themselves, so they're looking for turnkey solutions.

'They like a lot of natural fabrics and solid floors, with marble very much in demand,' he adds. 'White bathrooms and functional kitchens with lots of black lacquer are popular. Also, lots of big fashion houses are doing ranges of furniture so we'll buy into that – whether it's Fendi, Calvin Klein or Ralph Lauren – but then have their own furniture made to complement that. In a way interiors are taking over from clothes as an annual fashion. One year there will be a lot of chinchilla and wooden beds, another year there might be a lot of crystal or chenille. Swarovski seems to be the thing at the moment.'

Even as house prices across the UK headed downhill in 2008, Russian billionaire money piled into upmarket London property. In February 2008 Viktor Pinchuk, a Ukrainian businessman, bought a ten-bedroom house in Kensington for £80 million. In May, the Russian mining and metals billionaire Alisher Usmanov, who owns 25 per cent of Arsenal football club, paid £48 million for a house in Hampstead. In the first seven months of 2009, the capital saw 26 £10 million-plus homes sold while in October 2009 high-end estate agent Knight Frank handled four £10 million-plus sales to Russian and Chinese buyers, three in Belgravia for £16.25 million, £17 million and £32 million respectively and one in Knightsbridge for £11.5 million.

In 2007, Davies purchased Number 11 Cadogan Gardens, a leading boutique hotel, and set about redesigning it to act as a showcase for his interiors. It would have private suites, personal butlers, valet parking, Rolls-Royce Phantoms and Aston

Martins as well as arranged pick-ups for corporate jets flying in and out of London. At about the same time, Max Eaglen at Platform converted a mansion home on the Kings Road for the daughter of a Russian oligarch and found Tresserra furniture and a Minoti kitchen top of her list. 'It was the detail that proved crucial,' he explains. 'The flashy ostentatious trimmings of ten years ago have gone, so gold taps are a no-no. Instead, they wanted a £15,000 platinum finish tap that you could almost mistake for chrome until you got a little closer. They also wanted a softer finish to the apartment – even though it had a masculine feel. Ten years ago the finish would have been stark and hard.'

'Clients want a look to extend across all of their possessions,' argues Nick Candy, chief executive of Candy and Candy – a company owned by Nick and his brother Christian, which specializes in property for the super-rich. 'They want their jet, their helicopter, their boat and their apartment to follow the same design theme. Seventy per cent of that will [be] completely bespoke – whether it's Tom Ford doing bespoke or someone else – and they'll want a certain amount of discretion. It's not like a Gucci bag with a big G, more like a crocodile Hermès bag that everyone knows but doesn't scream tacky.'

This idea of an individual as a brand, creating a bespoke look for each of their homes, their yacht and their aircraft, means designers are starting to find it necessary to have a presence in all sectors. Versace has recently introduced a design service for private jet owners through TAG Group, parent company of TAG Aviation, based around a signature armchair from the Italian giant's home couture collection. The company's first contract is for a luxury interior comprising salon, galley, office, state-room and bathroom in an A319-based Airbus Corporate Jet, which will accommodate up to 16 passengers. All armchairs will be embossed with Versace's signature Greek fret motif.

Meanwhile Paul Priestman at Priestman Goode has recently finished the interior for the company's first private jet, creating a template design for Embraer's Lineage 1000, a jet worth roughly $50 million. Priestman explains that the challenge was the need for a bespoke service for clients who didn't want to wait a bespoke time frame. As a result, the interior is based on a modular design, so that buyers can choose an individual layout – the number of bedrooms, the configuration of rooms etc. – and Embraer can assemble their choice at speed. The component parts have a very clean, futuristic aesthetic. Lighting plays an important part, he explains, with stars projected on the ceilings and LEDs woven into the fabric of carpets and the seating or built into window panels. Priestman argues this supports Eaglen's comfort contention. 'When you walk on to most jets, you arrive at the galley and the toilet,' he explains. 'We designed an entrance hall with a seating area for people to take off their shoes and coats. Every inch of the service has to be discreet and comfortable so that people know they're getting something most people couldn't begin to pay for.'

The one area in which designers haven't yet been asked to express themselves is car interiors. Although Ferrari, Range Rover and Bentley retain their popularity and Aston Martin currently boasts the longest waiting list – 12 months and counting – Priestman, Davies and Candy believe the ubiquity of motoring means clients see them merely as tools or toys. 'Perhaps the future for designers,' says Nick Candy, 'is actually in creating bespoke cars for individual clients. I think that's got to be the next step.'

These billionaires take their tables at Cipriani while the paparazzi kick their heels outside, fully aware of their impact. Take R. Her husband has his own private jet waiting at Stansted, owns two London properties and divides his time equally

between the UK and Moscow. She e-mailed me an account of
her fellow Russians on a shopping trip:

> Anyone who has stumbled into the Knightsbridge radius
> knows we love to flash. Cars, clothes and jewellery . . . the
> bigger and the louder the better. The normal mundane and
> traditional English institutions get overwhelmed, I guess.
> Ridiculously expensive cars gridlocked on the tiny streets
> surrounding our local hot spots from Park Lane to Sloane
> Street . . . Herds of women forming colourful gangs adorned
> with so much bling and flash [it's] bright enough to make
> you cover your eyes with shades on an otherwise dreary
> London summer's day. . . . And boy when we come you
> know it. We couldn't survive without a clamber of assistants
> and staff to help us on a holiday, and look after our cutely
> co-ordinated Burberry-wearing kids who sometimes, with
> their parents, forget their manners back home; perhaps it
> is because we naively think our host country's fine citizens
> will overlook this for our hefty bank balances. However . . .
> my discussions with many disgruntled cab drivers, patient
> waiters and obliging sales [assistants reveal] . . . otherwise
> . . . Obviously, they are more appalled than in awe of our
> money-hungry ways . . . who would have guessed it?
>
> Is our well-known ambience less flashy and getting
> a bit trashy even by our own standards? As a relatively
> new mother I have a natural inclination to provide my son
> with the best I can possibly give him. [And I'm] fortunate
> enough to know that a well-rounded individual is not
> someone who knows the interior of a Rolls-Royce Phantom
> or one who has a Virtue phone lying in the bottom of a new
> crocodile Birkin bag . . .
>
> However, it seems on our way to becoming developed
> countries we left behind the important things in life and

settled comfortably into the luck which was bestowed upon us, dusting off the earth that gave us our riches to reside among as many new and expensive 'things' as possible. Desperately hoping they will elicit awe from anyone looking, without taking a bit of time for ourselves to grow and truly enrich our lives with things that no amount of money can buy.

The next time you see our theatrical shows where we cluster around our designated meeting points to show off ridiculous amounts of money, spending in a rather sombre economic climate, please don't judge us too harshly, just be sure to know we are just living out our nouveau riche status and sure enough in time we will catch on. Hey, if P. Diddy saw the elegance in sporting less ice around his neck for a more subtle touch of bling and felt secure enough in his status to, dare I say, fly commercial flights, surely there is hope for us.

According to Stephen O'Sullivan, who spent nine years in Russia with United Financial Group:

Russians have been in London for some time because it's close to Moscow and it's very international. London is an attractive market to them. Companies from the CIS [Commonwealth of Independent States] form an ever-greater part of the London stock market and Russian oligarchs are increasingly invested in it themselves through investment funds. Many of them practically operate as large institutions in their own right, playing the stock market, so they do have an enormous amount of influence – more so than previously – and I'm not sure everyone appreciates that.[1]

There is of course another reason for their presence: their

need for safe refuge. Litvinenko's pallbearer and wealthy industrialist Boris Berezovksy, for instance, fled to London shortly after Vladimir Putin took power in 2000. With his friend and fellow founding oligarch Mikhail Khodorkovsky in jail he feared a similar fate awaited him if he stayed in Moscow. Since arriving he has indeed fought off various extradition attempts from the Russian authorities. But why would the Russian state go to war with its richest citizens in these post-Communist days?

The answer lies in these billionaires' route from rags to riches. The story has been told before but to understand the rise of the world's oligarchs, it's important to understand how a small group of Russians emerged from the collapse of the Soviet Union to claim ownership of some of the world's most valuable petroleum, natural gas and metal deposits – resulting in one of the greatest transfers of wealth ever seen.

In 1990, Russia had not a single billionaire. By 1997, *Forbes* magazine's list of the world's richest billionaires boasted five Russians. By 2003, there were 17 billionaires; only Germany, Japan and the United States had more. Like many of the super-rich in this book, the Russian oligarchs were in an incredible place at an incredible time – but so were 140 million other people. Their success began, ironically, with Mikhail Gorbachev's attempts to save Communism.

Gorbachev was elected General Secretary of the Communist Party in 1985 and rapidly realized the system was in peril. Shortly after taking office, he publicly declared that the Soviet economy had stalled and was in desperate need of vigorous reorganization. If industrial and agricultural productivity were to rise, there had to be massive and rapid technological modernization as well as a significant reform of the clunky Soviet bureaucracy.

In 1986, therefore, he introduced two laws: the first allowing people to set up as self-employed entrepreneurs and the second paving the way for small businesses known as co-operatives. These co-operatives were, initially, only able to work in rigidly defined areas – recycling, baking, shoe repair, laundry services and consumer goods.

A thriving black market had been operating for years under Communism – usually referred to by ordinary Russians as *svyazi*, or connections. This black market crossed over with the more dubious activities of Russia's criminal class. Some hard-to-get items – like PCs – entered the Soviet Union via the same routes as illicit drugs or banned videos. All the same, a small group of idealists – including Anatoly Chubais and Yegor Gaidar, two of Russia's Young Reformers movement – and a slightly larger group of well-placed, quick-thinking wheeler-dealers – Boris Berezovsky, Mikhail Khodorkovsky, Mikhail Fridman, Vladimir Gusinsky, Vitaly Malkin, Vladimir Potanin, Alexander Smolensky, Oleg Deripaska, Mikhail Prokhorov and Roman Abramovich – used black market strategies and the economic changes of perestroika to their considerable advantage.

The first to really cash in were Khodorkovsky and Berezovsky. Khodorkovsky was the deputy head of the Communist youth movement known as Komsomol. Another Komsomol leader and good friend Alexei Golubovich had parents in senior positions in the State Bank of the USSR and together they used Komsomol's recognized authority to open a private café in 1986. The following year they took advantage of a law allowing Youth Science and Technology Centres to operate as businesses with an ultra-low 3 per cent tax rate. Khodorkovsky used the centre to start importing computers, then other highly demanded essentials like vodka and brandy.

He also worked a complex system of internal financing between state enterprises that used a kind of virtual currency – known as *beznalichnye* – to create one of Russia's first privately owned banks, Bank Menatep, in 1988. Menatep won the contract to distribute the compensation granted to the victims of the Chernobyl nuclear meltdown, and this helped underwrite a massive expansion of Khodorkovsky's import–export business.

Berezovsky, on the other hand, made his early money from automobiles. He started off selling software, then graduated to cars, importing second-hand Mercedes from East Germany, before setting up a curious car dealership called LogoVaz which, thanks to his connections at the Lada factory in Togliatti, gave him effective control over the car's distribution. He set up Mercedes, Fiat and Volvo dealerships and even entered a brief joint venture with General Motors to build a cheap Russian car – which would ultimately prove to be his downfall. His 'people's car' somehow never rolled off the assembly line, despite down payments from Russian citizens. This made him extremely unpopular – and something of an easy target. He also established a bank – United Bank – to finance his operations.

Others in the first wave of money-making took similar routes: Gusinsky drove a cab, made women's clothing and offered advice to foreign investors; Potanin used his family connections to set up a consulting firm and later become owner of Russia's largest private bank; Malkin was in construction; Fridman sold black market theatre tickets and cleaned windows; Vladimir Vinogradov parlayed his position as a State Bank employee to make his way into a private bank, while Alexander Smolensky printed business cards.

Under Communism, locally drilled oil and locally mined metals and minerals were sold internally at a massive discount against the world price. Many of those with newly acquired wealth spotted a unique opportunity and started trading locally acquired natural resources – bought cheap – on the international market to take advantage of the huge price difference. Some had well-connected state officials help them out while the most successful entrepreneurs forged links with high-level government functionaries and sympathetic politicians. All were on their way to serious wealth when, in 1991, a cabal of hard-line Communists mounted a coup in a bid to reverse Gorbachev's reforms. The coup's leaders ordered tanks to surround the Russian parliament, but hadn't counted on resistance in the form of Russian president Boris Yeltsin – who climbed on top of one tank and shouted defiance, encouraging massive street protests. Gradually the coup collapsed. Within 48 hours the plotters were on the run and, four months later, the Soviet Union was dissolved.

Yeltsin – a canny politician but poor economist – accelerated reforms but parcelled out the privatization of Russia's state-owned industries to his deputy for economic policy, the dissident economist Anatoly Chubais. Inspired by a similar scheme in Czechoslovakia, Chubais decided, essentially, to give away a significant stake in the factories, mines, yards and power stations. He issued 148 million vouchers for shares in state companies. The plan was to pull the Russian people behind privatization and thus behind Yeltsin. Initially it worked.

Handsomely printed in a rich brown with an etching of the Russian White House, the vouchers became the story of the year. Evening news programmes sent reporters into the streets to vox pop passers-by, asking what they planned to do with their voucher allowance. They were traded on Moscow's nascent commodity exchanges or bought and sold at news-stands and subway stations by the equivalent of ticket touts. Many were swapped for bottles of vodka. Others were scooped up by so-called 'Voucher Funds': often a front for factory managers wishing to buy their old company back or Mafia moneymen looking to launder money and gain economic muscle. Within months the vast majority of the vouchers had been sold for cash to these brokers. Naturally the oligarchs did very well, acquiring healthy stakes in various industries and, realizing the value of PR, starting to diversify – setting up TV stations and newspapers to spread their faith in the free market.

They started living hard and partying slightly harder. One American banker recalls heading for a meeting with a Russian tycoon in the late 1990s as Western banks scrabbled to be part of Russia's insane expansion. A Soviet ZIL limousine picked him up from his hotel and drove him to a large house on the outskirts of Moscow. Two armed men stood at the door. One of them let him in and he passed through a series of baroque chambers, each one with burly men standing like sentries either side of his next entrance. Finally he reached the meeting-room where the tycoon sat behind a large wooden table, with a muscular bodyguard hovering behind him.

The meeting began well, but started to deteriorate when the gulf between the kinds of assurances the banker was used to receiving clashed with the freewheeling Russian style. At one point the banker said, using an unfortunate but unconsciously chosen turn of phrase, 'Look, you're going have to bite the bullet on this one and accept—'

The tycoon interrupted him. 'No my friend,' his face was cold and unsmiling. 'It is you who will have to bite the bullet.'

'I was a bit freaked out by the way he said that, but the meeting went on for a little while longer,' the banker explains:

> In the end we didn't reach any conclusion, so I got ready to leave. At that point, the associate said, 'Excuse me, I don't think I have your business card.' I fished one out and gave it to him and he smiled and keeping his eyes on mine throughout, took the card, didn't even glance at it and handed it over his shoulder to his bodyguard who scrutinized it, then looked up and grinned at me. I'm sure it was just theatricalities but I wasn't taking the risk – I've got two kids – so I went back to the airport, phoned the

bank and told them to get me on the next flight home. I just stayed in the hotel until the flight left. That was the last time I did business in Russia.

Outside the boardroom, Russia's wealthy were equally imposing. Berezovsky's flamboyance is now the stuff of media legend. One former staff member, who worked at his mansion on Cap d'Antibes, recalls that the cellar was stocked with only two wines, one red and one white. The red was a Château Haut-Brion that retailed at $2,000 a bottle, while the white was a little more modest at $1,500 a bottle. The likes of Rupert Murdoch would drop by for lunch and eat sumptuously from menus whipped up at short notice by a huge team of chefs, although Berezovsky's mother would eat only variations on root vegetables, sending the kitchen mad trying to find different carrot-based dishes.

'The boss could be wildly generous, handing out $10,000-tips after spending the week at the World Cup in France, but he was also paranoid,' explains the ex-employee. 'Guys could be told to pack their things and leave at a moment's notice if he suspected them of anything less than full loyalty.' His paranoia also expressed itself in more obvious ways. The house had a full-time security team of 15 former Russian special forces, armed with snub-nosed machine guns – 'Although some were often stoned,' the employee recalls. 'They'd come out of their sentry hut with this glazed look on their faces with the smell of weed kind of hanging off them.'

The need for security wasn't entirely based on paranoia. During this employee's tenure, there were two raids on the house, one by the local police who fielded some 300 armed cops in a quick and brutally efficient sweep of the premises, and another by forces unknown who arrived en masse in the middle of the night sparking a full-scale gun battle that lasted some 15 minutes.

According to the burgeoning private security industry, this sort of thing is increasingly common in the playgrounds of the super-rich. Sascha Kunkel, a heavily built Bavarian ex-French Foreign Legionnaire and director general of the private security company ALGIZ Services, operates close protection teams on the Côte d'Azur:

> Everybody says the Côte d'Azur is safe and it is safe, it's not a Third World War raging. But there is potential threat – depending on the client. You have every Mafia of the world with a little cell there. These Mafias do their business in the[ir own] countries, obviously and if they have problems at home they are always protected up to the teeth. But if they go on holidays or to [a] second house they are vulnerable.

In fact, the oligarchs were also vulnerable to another threat – back at home the Russian people were starting to feel conned. The early-1990s economy was struggling. Yeltsin had ordered the liberalization of foreign trade, prices and currency, while raising interest rates to fight inflation. In early 1992, prices skyrocketed and a deep credit crunch shut down many industries, bringing about a protracted depression. Investors started to move money abroad, with an estimated $1 billion per month leaving the country. Russian and some Western economists blamed Yeltsin's economic programme for the country's disastrous economic performance. Many politicians began to distance themselves from him.

By 1995, the Russian government was in desperate need of funds so Yeltsin prepared for a new wave of privatization, offering shares in some of Russia's most valuable state enterprises in exchange for bank loans. The programme was promoted as a way of speeding up privatization while ensuring

the government a much-needed infusion of cash for its operating needs.

The scheme was the brainchild of Vladimir Potanin,
raised among the Russian nomenklatura and now owner of
Uneximbank. Banks provided the state with loans, taking shares
in state-owned companies, including some of the most valuable
oil and metal firms, as collateral. If the state could not repay
its loans, the bankers could auction off the shares themselves,
which is exactly what happened. In many cases, the auctions
were rigged and the auctioneers – the bankers – bought the
companies themselves at a price only slightly above the value
of the loans. Thus Mikhail Khodorkovsky gained control of oil
giant Yukos for a mere $300 million when the company was
actually worth $10 billion.

If Yeltsin hoped the loans-for-shares scheme would stabilize
the country, he was badly misguided. Those who were unable to
adapt quickly suffered. In particular, those employed by the
state – including teachers, doctors, professors and policemen
– learned to hate the 'new Russians' who were flocking to the
newly opened restaurants, night clubs and casinos. The dis-
parity of wealth sparked a powerful revival of the Communists.
In February 1996, Yeltsin announced he would seek a second
term as president, amid weeks of speculation over his health
problems and growing unpopularity in Russia. When campaigning opened, his popularity was close to zero. Meanwhile
the Communist Party, and its candidate Gennady Zyuganov,
was playing to memories of Soviet prestige and domestic order.

At the World Economic Forum in Davos, Switzerland in
February 1996, Zyuganov gave interviews and press confer-
ences portraying himself as a Western-friendly modernizing
Communist, vastly impressing the bankers, businessmen
and political leaders gathered there, as Emily L. Walker, then
in charge of US banking giant Citibank's emerging markets

department, recalls: 'Zyuganov pretty much stole the show and the impression you got was that the West was ready to receive him.'

Panic struck the Yeltsin team and he appointed Chubais as his campaign manager. Chubais swiftly gathered a group of seven oligarchs – Berezovsky, Gusinsky, Khodorkovsky, Potanin, Vinogradov, Smolensky and Fridman – to save Yeltsin's campaign. They held a late-night meeting with Yeltsin where they outlined their proposals. They would mastermind and bankroll his campaign, using their television and newspaper companies as presidential propaganda machines to enormous effect.

Berezovsky, for instance, was now running Russia's main TV station – Obshchestvennoe Rossiyskoye Televidenie's (ORT) Channel One – while Gusinsky owned NTV, the newspaper *Segodnya* and various magazines. Both channels were devoted to Yeltsin's cause. The oligarchs launched a newspaper called *God Forbid*, sent to 10 million Russian homes, which carried an endless stream of anti-Zyuganov articles. They concealed Yeltsin's heart attack mid-campaign, broadcasting a specially doctored tape of one of his speeches. Overall Yeltsin's campaign, under campaign rules, had an official budget of $3 million, but it actually spent closer to $100 million.

With this support, Boris went from 5 per cent in the polls to outright victory. The super-rich had become true oligarchs with position and influence within the government. Foolishly, a confident Berezovsky gave a post-election interview with the *Financial Times* in which he said seven tycoons controlled 50 per cent of the Russian economy. 'I think that two types of power are possible,' he told David Hoffman. 'Either a power of ideology or a power of capital. Ideology is now dead. I think that if something is advantageous to capital it is advantageous to the nation.'[2] Other, smaller, regional oligarchs started establishing local empires. Insider dealing was commonplace.

Economist Lev Timofeev was appalled:

> There is no longer a real need for making any special effort to 'launder' dirty money in Russia under the prevailing conditions of widespread corruption and shadow [sic] economic relations. There is no urgent need for legalizing ill-gotten capital as it can be directly employed for acquiring factories, oil companies, mineral deposits and, what is most significant (and most alarming for us), for buying influence with the legislative bodies and executive governmental agencies, with the regional administration officials, with the men running the national economy, with the commanders of the armed forces, and so on. Ultimately, it is possible to buy out all the levers controlling the destiny of the entire nation.[3]

Ironically, the oligarch's finest piece of political jostling would prove the most dangerous: persuading Yeltsin to appoint Vladimir Putin as his successor. It was Berezovky's idea. In 1998 he became worried about what he called 'the continuity of power' – he felt it was essential to secure a leader with Yeltsin's view of the benefits of the oligarchy. Moscow mayor Yuri Luzhkov and former premier Yevgeny Primakov – both highly critical of the oligarchs – had already declared their intention to run. This didn't suit the oligarchs at all. Vladimir Putin, a former KGB man who was now Yeltsin's fourth prime minister, seemed a far better prospect. In 1998 and 1999, Spanish police mounting a surveillance operation on a suspected Russian mobster in the Andalusian super-rich resort Sotogrande saw Putin visit the mobster's neighbour Berezovksy five times – flying into nearby Gibraltar, then taking a boat along the coast to Sotogrande's marina – as the two created Unity, Putin's political party. Finally, Yeltsin resigned at the end of 1999 and appointed Putin acting president. The rest was a shoo-in. Sort of.

On a cold day in October 2003 Mikhail Khodorkovsky, then Russia's richest man, gathered a small group of senior executives from Yukos, his sprawling oil behemoth, in a rustic-themed Russian restaurant in St Petersburg. Vodka flowed freely and, as at all large Russian meals, the time soon came for the toasts. These can be a brutal experience for the casual drinker. Each member of the party makes an elaborate toast to their host. Everybody drinks. The host returns the honour. Everybody drinks. And so to the next person at the table.

On this occasion Ray Leonard, an American geologist who ran Yukos's exploration department, raised his glass to Khodorkovsky and lavished extensive praise on his boss:

> 'This is the first time I have been to St Petersburg with Mikhail Borisovich,' he said. 'I have been reading a biography of Peter the Great. Peter the Great invited foreigners in and had to defend them against the locals. Three hundred years later, not that much has changed. Yukos is a small microcosm of the same process and I am proud to be a small part of it.'

Khodorkovsky, whose personal wealth was then estimated at around $8 billion, replied with strangely prophetic words:

> We have to remember that under Peter the Great there were 24 million Russians and 300,000 of them died building St Petersburg. There were 2 million fewer Russians when Peter the Great died than there had been when he became tsar. We have developed quickly, and we have developed slowly, but in all this time, human life in Russia has not been worth even a kopek.[4]

Barely a month later, on 25 October, armed police stopped Khodorkovsky as he attempted to board a plane at Novosibirsk airport, arresting him for fraud and tax evasion. He was taken at gunpoint to Moscow's brutally overcrowded Matrosskaya Tishina prison. The news stunned the business world and prices on the Russian stock market went into freefall until the market was briefly closed to prevent further drops. Then, on 31 October, Vladimir Putin's government froze Yukos's shares.

At his trial Khodorkovsky was accused of dubious share deals during the wave of privatizations that swept Russia in 1994 on top of the threatened tax-evasion and fraud charges. He was also investigated over four murders, allegedly carried out with the complicity of Yukos's board. He was jailed for eight years – soon to be extended to 15.

Khodorkovsky couldn't say he hadn't been warned. As soon as Vladimir Putin succeeded Boris Yeltsin he had confronted the half-dozen oligarchs who controlled the heights of the Russian economy. He had summoned them for a meeting in the Kremlin to announce a new deal: they could keep the vast resources they had acquired during the Yeltsin era, but they would no longer be allowed to play any sort of role in politics.

'Putin wanted to show the oligarchs that if they wanted to keep on making money, they would have to be loyal,' according to one Kremlin-watching, Moscow-based banker. 'He was aware of how much Yeltsin depended on the oligarchs and he wanted to make it clear things had changed. His message was: if you're not loyal, you're in prison.' So clear were the warnings that two of the players – Vladimir Gusinsky and Boris Berezovsky – had taken the hint and fled the country; Gusinsky to Israel and Berezovsky to London where he formed a circle of émigrés, fought extradition for fraud and money laundering and – in various interviews with UK newspapers – called for a coup against Putin.

Khodorkovsky had stayed and initially prospered but had carried on donating to the progressive political parties Yabloko and the Union of Right Forces. In 2003, he had engineered Russia's largest merger, joining Yukos with Roman Ambramovich's oil company Sibneft. He'd begun negotiations with ExxonMobil and ChevronTexaco about selling a stake in the combined enterprise for $25 billion. Then he'd started questioning the Kremlin about a deal he believed to be corrupt, involving the state-owned oil company Rosneft. A counter-campaign of smears and investigations had begun immediately – ending in his arrest.

There were those who thought he had had it coming. Bill Browder, an American fund manager who had been working in Russia for a decade, told the *Financial Times*: 'A nice, well-run authoritarian regime is better than an oligarchic Mafia regime – and those are the choices on offer.'[5] And so, observers thought, Russia entered a period dominated by the rule of law – a heavy-handed law, perhaps, a law as interpreted by a former KGB apparatchik, sure. But law none the less. The chaos of the 'anything goes' 1990s was over. There were even those who expected the loans-for-shares scandal to be reversed. Surely, the argument went, the oligarchs were finished? Recent events, however, have proved the opposite. They have proved that it all depends what kind of oligarch you are.

CHAPTER TWO

IN WHICH PUTIN BARKS BUT
DOESN'T BITE

Meiendorf Castle is an old tsarist-era hunting lodge just outside Moscow. It sits in the heart of a thick forest and, built to look like a German medieval castle, it has a certain fairy-tale feel. In the new Russia, Meiendorf is a presidential residence – the one favoured for high-level international summits and hosting foreign leaders. In November 2008, however, it was the scene of a different kind of summit – one that proved the power and the money were cosier than ever before.

Russia's richest men arrived at the meeting in chauffeur-driven Bentleys, BMWs and Maybachs – as usual, surrounded by a phalanx of bodyguards. They filed through the castle's gothic splendour and took their seats in an oak-panelled dining-room. Armed police sealed off a 25-mile (40-kilometre) road from the Kremlin to the castle so that president Dmitry Medvedev's motorcade could hurtle to the rendezvous.[1] Medvedev insisted the meeting was an informal dinner to discuss the world's financial crisis with the country's surviving oligarchs, a surprisingly large group of youngish men – still in their forties – but considerably poorer than they had been six months previously. Since May the country's stock market had fallen by 80 per cent. According to one calculation, Russia's tycoons had lost close to £150 billion.

At the dinner, and over the following months, the Russian state agreed to loan billions of dollars to its wealthiest sons and work as hard as possible to prevent them losing their fortunes. For the Russia-watchers who had predicted the end of the billionaire class, this was more than unexpected – most news organizations had spent the previous five years predicting their imminent downfall at the hands of an angry Kremlin. According to the *Financial Times* Moscow correspondent Charles Clover:

> Everyone expected that when the oligarchs took state loans and when the loans fell due in autumn 2009 the Kremlin might try a 'loans-for-shares' takeover in reverse. The state would either take over or bankrupt the companies. Russian bankruptcy law is brutal – you can go after a $50 million company with a $5 debt and with a friendly judge you can gain control. But that hasn't happened. It's a clear sign that the redistribution of property has stopped.

When the state chose not to renationalize, it was clear that Russia's super-rich were no longer outsiders. Quite the opposite. They were effectively emissaries of Russia's aggressive desire for economic expansion and modernization. In deal after deal, the Kremlin backed the oligarchs – most particularly when it came to taking on the West.

There had been clues earlier in the year, during the bizarre boardroom battle for control of the joint Anglo-Russian oil company TNK-BP. In 2003, the same year Putin clamped down so heavily on Khodorkovsky's Yukos – ultimately selling its choice assets to the state-owned Rosneft – the oligarchs Mikhail Fridman, German Khan, Viktor Vekselberg and Len Blavatnik had sold half of their Alfa Access/Renova Group (AAR) subsidiary Tyuman Oil to BP for $6.15 billion. Tony Blair and Vladimir Putin witnessed the signing of the deal as part of a blaze of publicity, creating the large joint venture.

TNK-BP had seemed like the answer to some aggressive oligarch jostling during the old Yeltsin era. The idea of a formal arrangement between Fridman's AAR and respectable BP seemed to signify a change of heart and possibly herald an era of mutual trust. In the late 1990s, BP had nearly lost its $500 million investment in Russian oil when the oligarchs took advantage of the country's weak courts to seize the assets of a BP-owned company. Lord Browne of Madingley, BP's chief executive at the time of the deal, had fought Fridman's attempt to take assets cheaply out of Sidanco, a Russian oil group in which BP had a 10 per cent stake, using his connections in America and Downing Street. He had effectively orchestrated a campaign to block banks from financing the deal on corruption grounds.

After Putin came to power in 2000 and began reasserting Kremlin authority, the same oligarchs had come to BP looking for a deal they hoped would protect them from partial nationalizations like Yukos. In 2003, BP had swallowed its reservations about the oligarchs and did the deal.

TNK-BP accounted for a quarter of BP's production and a fifth of its reserves. Dividend payment from the joint venture – and the respectability afforded by the BP tie-in – meant that by 2008 AAR's billionaires had received $18 billion between them. This had funded their forays into industries around the world and allowed them to forge important contacts in government and industry. Blavatnik's Access Industries (AI) conglomerate has key relationships with some of the biggest names in international finance. Fridman is an adviser to the Council on Foreign

Relations, the influential New York think tank. Douglas Hurd, the former Tory MP, sits on the board of Altimo, a company owned by Fridman's AAR. Lord Powell, Margaret Thatcher's adviser on foreign affairs, sits on the advisory board of asset management company Alfa Capital, another AAR subsidiary. So when TNK-BP's head – veteran oilman Bob Dudley – fled Russia and went into hiding in July 2008, it came as something of a blow to those who had hoped the oligarchs were changing their ways.

Things had been unravelling for a while. Among other things, Fridman was keen to pursue deals in countries the West has sanctions against or trading problems with – including Sudan, North Korea, Syria, Iran and Myanmar. BP objected. On 19 March 2008 and then again on 20 May BP's Moscow offices were raided by the FSB; TNK-BP's offices had been inspected four times by the labour ministry; a former employee had been arrested on charges of industrial espionage; in June Dudley had been interrogated for six hours at the Ministry of Internal Affairs over possible tax-avoidance schemes that may have taken place at TNK back in 2001 – two years before he arrived; Khan, Fridman's colleague at AAR, who was responsible for government relations at TNK-BP, had ignored a request from Dudley for 150 visa renewals for foreign staff – instead requesting just 63 from immigration authorities and thus, in effect, ending the employment of nearly half the company's technical specialists. At one point, TNK-BP security men denied BP staff entry to TNK-BP headquarters.

Mississippi-born Dudley's office was so heavily bugged he had had to stand on his office balcony to make mobile phone calls. Just five days before he left, when his temporary work visa expired, there had been hope that he would be able to obtain a new one. Instead, he had booked a flight and headed for a secret location. BP went to extraordinary lengths to conceal his whereabouts, using complex technology to keep his phone calls and e-mails untraceable.

Peter Sutherland, the BP chairman, used a June press conference in Stockholm to lament the government's lack of action to halt the oligarchy's strong-arm tactics. 'This is just a return to the corporate raiding activities that were prevalent in Russia in the 1990s,' he insisted. 'Prime Minister Putin has referred to these tactics as relics of the 1990s, but unfortunately our partners continue to use them.'

BP's problem, according to oil industry experts, was that it thought there was a new Russia – oligarchs out, state-owned enterprises in – when really nothing had changed. In 2007 Gazprom and BP had appeared to be heading towards a new deal. Gazprom had indicated it might buy out the AAR group oligarchs and BP believed that a deal would cement its position as the dominant foreign player in Russian oil. They hadn't reckoned on Mikhail Fridman.

A native of Ukraine who'd grown up listening to Radio Liberty, Fridman was 17 when he moved to Moscow as an impoverished student. He started out in business under Communism by bartering theatre tickets for goods on the black market. He later founded one of the Soviet Union's early private businesses, trying everything – even breeding laboratory mice – until he started a window-cleaning company. By 1991 he was a dollar millionaire. A few years later he joined in the feeding frenzy around Russia's mass privatization. He recruited Pyotr Aven, Yeltsin's first Trade Minister, who later became an oligarch in his own right, and together they won government contracts and oil export licences. More importantly, back in 1992, when Aven had been Minister for External Economic Relations he had come into close contact with one of his underlings in St Petersburg's city hall: a former KGB colonel responsible for attracting foreign investment, one Vladimir Putin.

According to one investment banker:

> Gazprom approached BP to talk about Alfa's TNK stake in
> the summer of 2007. As soon as Fridman heard about this
> he went to Putin and said 'Vladimir Vladovich, is this your
> desire?' Putin said no. And that was that. Fridman went for
> BP with everything he had. Oligarchs have what they call
> 'Administrative Resources' – friendly judges, officials and
> so forth. The tools of the Russian state. That can hurt. BP
> misread the political situation. The sun is not setting on
> the oligarchs. This particular group of oligarchs has a very
> good relationship with the government.

Just after Bob Dudley's departure, Mikhail Fridman granted
a rare interview with the *Sunday Times*. 'Our demands are
reasonable,' he argued, before continuing:

> Ultimately the main problem is an emotional one. Since we
> are not professional oilmen, BP appears to have thought
> of us as oligarchs who became rich by chance as a result
> of the chaos of the 1990s. And that most of all we would
> be interested in having fun with yachts, private Boeings
> and football clubs. But we're very hands-on businessmen
> who take a keen interest in making sure our investments
> are as profitable as possible. TNK is our baby. We bought
> it when it was bankrupt and turned it into a success. We're
> not trying to take over anything. We want an independent
> company. And we'll succeed.'[2]

In May 2009, TNK-BP appointed Fridman as its interim CEO.
    The pattern is repeated across the board. Abramovich, for
instance, 'still enjoys a special relationship with the Kremlin',
according to a former Putin aide. 'He can be trusted to buy or

sell a business when asked by the Kremlin. He sticks to the rules of the game and pays his dues.'

'The Russians who make a lot of noise in the West are hardly considered in Moscow,' according to Quinn Martin at Moscow-based investment bank Renaissance Capital. 'The likes of Mikhail Fridman and Oleg Deripaska who stayed [i.e. kept homes here], who invested carefully and who didn't get political are far more important.'

Deripaska is the sole owner and CEO of Basic Element, which owns, among others, the world's largest aluminium company, Russian Aluminium or Rusal, Russia's oldest insurance company Ingosstrakh, Soyuz Bank, aircraft company Aiakor, energy company EuroSibEnergo and the Russian car company GAZ – with plants or subsidiaries on every continent. Although hampered by the credit crunch, his aggressive acquisition strategy returned with his bid, through GAZ, to buy General Motors' (GM) German car-maker Opel and its UK subsidiary Vauxhall. The deal fell through when GM withdrew, but Deripaska had clearly been a beneficiary of Kremlin support. Indeed, that may have helped stoke GM's fears.

Deripaska first came to the attention of most of the British public in August 2008 when he hosted a party on his yacht – its hull built in grey steel and with a white aluminium superstructure – the 236-foot (72-metre) *Queen K*, as it sat moored off the coast of the Greek island of Corfu. The guests included Peter Mandelson, then a European Union (EU) commissioner, and George Osborne, chief finance spokesman for the UK's opposition Conservative Party. The *Sunday Times* claimed that Osborne had tapped Deripaska for a donation to the Tory Party after being entertained on board. The paper also claimed that during the past three years Mandelson – as EU trade commissioner – had twice acted to cut European aluminium import duties and Deripaska's company Rusal had been one of the main beneficiaries.[3]

Both Osborne and Mandelson should have expected some sort of scandal. US presidential hopeful John McCain had to back-pedal furiously during his election campaign when the *Washington Post* revealed details of his meetings with Deripaska in Switzerland and Montenegro. In July 2009 Tory blogger Guido Fawkes made much of David Cameron dining with Roland Rudd, Deripaska's lobbyist.

Indeed, rumour and suspicion have dogged Deripaska since the very early days of his career. Until late 2005 he had been refused a US visa despite being a major industrialist. After hiring Bob Dole, the former presidential candidate and attorney, to plead his case he was finally granted a visa, but it was revoked in July 2006 as FBI officials believed Deripaska had not been 'candid with them about his past business dealings'.

Meanwhile, he has been fighting court cases on a seemingly annual basis. British businessmen Simon and David Reuben were originally in partnership with Deripaska but had to sell out, subsequently suing him and settling in 2005. Deripaska has also settled disputes with the Zhivilo brothers and Anatoly 'The Bull' Bykov – both had previously controlled valuable Siberian smelters – while several cases have been brought against him in US courts and been thrown out for lack of evidence or juris-diction. In November 2003 Mr Justice Jack found for Tekron Resources against Rusal in a dispute over a bauxite mine and refinery in the west African state of Guinea. In October 2005, Mr Justice Blackburne was highly critical of Rusal's role in a dispute over an aluminium smelter in Tajikistan.

Like all good oligarchs he has a house in London, a Grade I listed 11-bedroom Regency house on Belgrave Square, which he bought through a company registered in the British Virgin Islands in 2003 for £17 million. Built to entertain royalty, it boasts a sweeping staircase and opulent rococo reception rooms. He also owns a £7.1 million house in Surrey on St George's

Hill – the former Digger redoubt that has become a luxurious gated private estate with its own golf and tennis club and an average house price of around £3 million.

Although his two children are privately educated in London, Deripaska has homes in Russia – a top-floor apartment in Moscow's 'Golden Mile' where he added an extra floor in the face of residents' protests as well as a vast dacha in southern Siberia near a skiing resort – and his residential property empire includes three houses in France as well as residences in Sardinia, New Delhi, Beijing and Kiev. In familiar pattern, his opulent lifestyle belies, or arises from, his incredibly humble beginnings.

Deripaska was born in 1968 in Dzerzhinsk, 249 miles (400 kilometres) south of Moscow. The city – named after the first head of the Cheka, Lenin's secret police – was the centre of Russia's chemical industry and, as it counted as a strategic resource of the Soviet system, it spent many years as a closed city like the Black Sea fleet's port city Sevastopol, with check-points preventing outsiders from entering. After his father died when Oleg was four and the boy moved to Krasnodar, a small village in southern Russia, he was raised by his Cossack grandparents in a kind of rural idyll – milking cows and fetching water – while his engineer mother worked in another city.

Although his parents were Jewish, Deripaska prefers to reference his Cossack heritage – attributing, in one interview, his business skills to the nomadic warrior bloodline: 'We Cossacks . . . are always prepared for war. It's a question of being able to deal with . . . every situation.'[4]

Soviet Russia had little time for either Cossacks or Jews, however, suspecting both of anti-Soviet sympathies. When Deripaska's grandparents died – he was aged seven at the time – the state seized the farm as part of a policy of breaking up

Cossack settlements. Young Oleg was passed from one relative to another until he was finally reunited with his mother when he was a teenager.

After conscription – he was stationed on a barren steppe on the Chinese border – he started but failed to finish a degree in quantum physics at Moscow State University. As with all the oligarchs, events overtook him. The collapse of the Soviet Union drained the reserves of the quiet Cossack farmers and Oleg had to work on building sites to earn enough money to eat. In the end, he gave up his studies and became a metals trader in Moscow. Initially he used his trading skills to build up stakes in emerging companies while the other oligarchs were preparing for the 'loans-for-shares' sell-off. In 1993, he travelled to a metals conference at the Dorchester Hotel in London where he met Mikhail Cherney, another rapidly rising force in the aluminium industry.

Mikhail and Oleg hit it off. According to many accounts, Mikhail was looking for a man he could trust to act on the ground in his slow takeover of Siberia's Sayanogorsky smelter and appointed Oleg as manager. In legal papers from a 2005 court case, the Reuben brothers claimed they brought in the young Mr Deripaska as an agent to buy up shares in the privatizations of Russia's giant Bratsk and Sayansk smelters, although Deripaska rapidly grew powerful in his own right by buying up his own shares until, by the end of 1994, the four men owned the plant between them.

By the time he got there in the mid-1990s, the aluminium industry was starting to get very ugly indeed. The former owners were preparing to try and retake the factory – a simple enough sentence, but in mid-1990s Russia, retake could mean many things. The Russian Mafia were trying to muscle in on the lucrative aluminium trade – almost every step of the process received generous tax breaks, meaning profit margins were huge – and violence was erupting in a series of disputes so bloody that they're still known as the 'Aluminium Wars'. Contract killings and extortion were part of day-to-day business – obviously without the knowledge or approval of any of the legitimate businessmen involved. According to Cherney, for instance, after a manager who had just signed a deal with him was beaten up, friends at a Moscow tennis club warned him, 'We've heard people want to kill you. You should leave.' Cherney emigrated to Israel in 1994, though he retained his Russian interests for some time longer.

The worst fighting in the Aluminium Wars was around the Krasnoyarsk plant in Siberia, the second largest in the country, with earnings of $1 billion a year. At one point the Krasnoyarsk plant changed hands literally with a keystroke when Cherney's 20 per cent stake was simply deleted by the plant's manager, claiming there had been something improper about the deal. The courts proved unable to help. During the Aluminium Wars, disputes were rarely settled by legal means.

Within weeks of the Krasnoyarsk share erasure a government supervisor for the metals sector died under the wheels of a car, as did plant manager Alexander Borisov, who had been involved in forging documents. Shortly after Oleg's appointment in 1994, a hired killer seriously wounded his financial director in a bungled assassination attempt. The director of a Rusal smelter nearby in Krasnoyarsk quit after being severely beaten in the doorway to his apartment. In April 1995 Vadim Yafyasov was sprayed with gunfire just weeks after being named a deputy director at the Krasnoyarsk plant. Not long after Yafyasov's funeral, the throat of Oleg Kantor, a banker with close business ties to the plant, was cut. As Richard Behar wrote in *Fortune* magazine in 2000, 'The recarving of the local aluminium market has been going on to the accompaniment of machine guns.'[5]

In 1997 Russia's Interior Minister, Anatoly Kulikov, linked the trouble in the aluminum trade – which accounted for 35 lives in 1995 alone – to the Izmailovo gang, which he claimed was being led by one Anton Malevsky. He added that mobsters controlled 'almost all' the deals in the Krasnoyarsk and Bratsk plants. Four days later, the campaigning journalist Vadim Birukov, whose magazine *Business in Russia* was the first independent title to expose organized crime's role in aluminum, was found dead in his garage, his body badly beaten and his mouth taped up as a warning to others who felt like talking. The culprits were never found.

Deripaska thus found himself effectively taking on the local Mafia in a battle for control. There is no shortage of stories of his being threatened by organized crime groups: at one point, Deripaska's enemies tried to ambush him on a mountain road with a grenade-launcher, and for a while he slept on the floor of the factory for safety, despite occasional attempts by armed gangs to raid the place.

Over time, protection rackets run by organized crime groups were taken on by Russia's various law enforcement agencies. Deripaska sided with the cops – as did Roman Abramovich, who had been making money as a street trader, a toy-maker and an oil broker before buying into aluminium factories in the late 1990s – although in court papers Roman credits a now dead Georgian oligarch, who also had his own interests in aluminium, Arkady 'Badri' Patarkatsishvili, for protecting him in the struggle in return for some $500 million.

Between them, by 2000, Deripaska and Abramovich had already taken control of over 70 per cent of the nation's aluminium output, when the former bosses of the large Kraz and Novokuznetsk smelters, who were facing jail, opted to sell their stakes to the duo.

In March 2000 Deripaska and Abramovich met Boris Berezovksy, who had a series of joint ventures with Abramovich including a joint stake in Sibneft, and the Georgian metals magnate 'Badri' Patarkatsishvili, at the Dorchester in London. Between them the four men owned the aluminium industry in Russia and they now agreed to merge all holdings into one powerful company – Russian Aluminium or Rusal. Two years later Deripaska bought out Abramovich for an estimated $2 billion. Roman also helped Oleg find something just as important in the long term – a wife with impeccable political connections. In 2000, Deripaska met Polina Yumashev, a friend of Abramovich's girlfriend Daria Zhukova, at Roman's apartment. While Oleg fell for Polina swiftly and was soon bombarding her with gifts in a sustained campaign to woo her, it's proved very helpful over the past few years that Polina, as step-granddaughter of Boris Yeltsin, offers access to an influential cadre of Kremlin advisers.

Meanwhile, relations between Deripaska and his mentor had deteriorated. In March 2001, the pair met at the Lanesborough Hotel in London to discuss Cherney's exit strategy from the aluminium industry – athough no longer living in Russia, he still had substantial investments there. By Cherney's account Deripaska 'panicked when he heard . . . that I was going to sell my stake in Rusal to MDM Bank for $1 billion. So I sold the stake to him instead, and the contract guaranteed payment in three years.' Then, according to Cherney, Deripaska paid $250 million and agreed to hold in trust a 20 per cent stake in Rusal which Oleg later refused to hand over. 'He met me in secret in Vienna in 2003 and I told him he had violated the terms,' says Cherney. 'Then he stopped answering the phone.'[6] Deripaska, however, maintains that there had never been an agreement either to hold any stake in trust or to transfer it to Cherney.

Cherney sued. At the initial hearing at London's Commercial Court in May 2007 – where Cherney sought to have the trial held in the UK and Deripaska tried to move the hearing to Russia – tantalizing details of Deripaska's London home, three houses in France, two Gulfstream jets, one Sikorsky helicopter and even the number of nights he spends in Moscow and London emerged. The judge's ruling included the fact that of the 33 nights he spent at the London home in 2006, just seven of them were shared with his wife. For Judge Langley, use of the Belgrave Square house 'is infrequent, intermittent, and generally fleeting', and nor is it a place where Deripaska runs his global metals and minerals business. 'The probability,' said the judge, 'is that in a real sense they [business affairs] are managed at the highest level by Mr Deripaska wherever he happens to be.' The headquarters of the world's largest aluminium company, in other words, are wherever Deripaska 'happens to be'.

Deripaska appealed and – in May 2008 – lost again. The ruling highlighted Oleg's importance to the Kremlin, as Mr Justice Christopher Clarke told the courtroom:

Mr Deripaska's Rusal group is one of the most important assets of the Russian economy and is of extraordinary importance to the Russian state and its project, under President Putin[,] of national revival involving, since 2004, increasing state control of key businesses, of which aluminium is one. It has been acknowledged at the highest level that there are problems of corruption in the judicial system and of political interference. Mr Deripaska is, by common account, a Kremlin-friendly oligarch, who heeded President Putin's warning to the oligarchs to stay out of politics. Others have found themselves in exile – Gusinsky, Berezovsky – or in a Siberian labour camp – Khodorkovsky of Yukos. But Mr Deripaska emerged as the triumphant leader of the Kremlin-friendly oligarchs whose ability to continue to do business is dependent on obedience to the Kremlin and who can count, in turn, on support from the government and the judicial system. He has funded President Putin's pet projects such as the construction of a new airport for the 2012 Winter Olympics. The available evidence indicates that Mr Cherney will not obtain a just and expeditious hearing in the Russian . . . courts and that there is a strong likelihood that he will be arrested on false allegations.[7]

As the downturn hit, it briefly appeared as if Deripaska's Kremlin connections had deserted him. Despite his cosy relationship with Putin – the former president visited Deripaska's ski retreat in Siberia – May 2009 saw the Russian Prime Minister launch a lacerating attack on the oligarch live on television, describing one of his factories as a 'rubbish dump' and saying he'd behaved appallingly to his workers.

In a scene still available to view on YouTube, Deripaska was called before Putin in Pikalyovo, a small town south of St Petersburg, where a quarter of the small town's population worked at one of Pikalyovo's three factories, two days after angry protesters from one of them – where he'd wound down operations because of the recession – blocked roads in fury over unpaid wages. Fearing that the unrest might spread, and keen to show that the wage arrears were the factory owner's fault, Putin demanded in a confrontation transmitted on national television that Deripaska pay the back wages. He tossed the oligarch a pen and told him to sign the order to start payment immediately. Deripaska signed.

For some observers, however, the significant event was the mysterious event of the dog in the night-time – the bark that didn't happen. 'At any time in 2008 or 2009 the Russian government could have nationalized Deripaska's empire, or indeed any of the oligarch's businesses,' according to Quinn Martin of Moscow-based Renaissance Capital. 'The fact that they didn't shows that old threats to the oligarchs have pretty much disappeared. In fact, it's quite the other way. Recent deals have shown that the oligarchs are not only essential to the Russian economy; they are essential to the Russian government. Their power can only grow.'

Behind the scenes, the Kremlin had been scrambling to save Deripaska. In 2008, Oleg's Rusal asked for the single largest loan in Moscow's bailout programme – $4.5 billion. He needed the money to avoid losing his stake in the mining giant Norilsk Nickel. As well as lending the money, the Kremlin applied pressure to other oligarchs to help Deripaska out.

First they turned to Mikhail Prokhorov, a flamboyant playboy who'd got incredibly lucky when the French police arrested him for pimping in 2007. He made his fortune at 30 with Vladimir Potanin when they won control of Norilsk as part of the loans-for-shares auctions and set about spending it with relish. He likes to party, kick-box and ski. In 2009 he threw a party on the battle cruiser *Aurora* during which, according to *Pravda* 'strong beverages made the guests lose control over themselves. Some of them decided to jump overboard to swim in the Neva River.'

In 2007 the young playboy was partying at the French ski resort Courchevel, seeing in the Russian Orthodox New Year as is the custom with Russia's newly minted, when the hooker scandal struck. His bash at the Hotel Byblos was in full swing when a team of 50 officers charged in and arrested 26 people, including the host – at that time chief executive of Norilsk Nickel and the 89th richest man in the world. The French accused him of flying in 16 Russian prostitutes to help his guests relax. Prokhorov told police that he brought the women over because he enjoyed the company of young, clever and beautiful female companions.

The case was not only dropped in 2009, but the French authorities issued an apology to Prokhorov. By then it had dealt Prokhorov an incredibly lucky hand. Potanin used the scandal to push him out of Norilsk. He forced Prokhorov to swap his shares for a stake in Deripaska's Rusal and about $7 billion in cash. This seemed like a harsh punishment, until the world economy crashed a few months later and it became clear he'd sold for 10 times what he could have obtained less than a year later. He was suddenly the richest man in Russia – worth $9.5 billion.

As part of the original forced sale, Prokhorov could have forced Deripaska to buy his shares in Rusal for around $275 in late 2009. At the time the sale came due, Norilsk was trading at $49.40. Prokhorov did not invoke his right to force the deal – giving Deripaska valuable breathing space.

The Kremlin stepped in again when Fridman tried to bankrupt Deripaska and thus gain control over Rusal. Fridman's AAR was the only lender that refused to join a debt restructuring agreement for Rusal. 'Doing deals with the Alfa Bank guys is hard,' explains one banker. 'You ask most people about repayments and they're happy to negotiate. AAR want 100 cents in the dollar.' Then Fridman tried to call in an overdue debt to force Rusal into bankruptcy.

Each surviving oligarch has powerful protectors and allies in the Kremlin. AAR – because Fridman's protector is his old friend Putin – is perceived to have the most powerful allies. Even so, the Kremlin said no. 'We don't want to see anything change hands due to bankruptcy,' one economic adviser to the Kremlin reports. 'It was a small debt, Rusal is being well run – they are using these factories properly, Deripaska is building cars. To split Rusal up would be dangerous. If you give part of it to Alfa Bank you break off the supply from factories in the Rusal Group, the supply chain ruptures, people lose jobs and everyone goes to war again.'

* * *

Why does this internal squabble matter? Take what almost happened with General Motors' attempted sale of its European arm – Opel and Vauxhall. Deripaska's GAZ car-maker initially led the Russian-backed consortium – which included Canadian car parts-maker Magna – that won the bidding war for Opel. Two weeks before the deal went through, however, the US government quietly told General Motors, in which it owns a controlling 60 per cent stake, not to sell to Deripaska. So GAZ dropped out and Magna and state-owned Russian bank Sberbank agreed a deal giving them a joint 55 per cent stake in Opel, with GM keeping 35 per cent.

Intriguingly, however, Sberbank head German Gref – who was Russia's Economy Minister for seven years – told *Vedomosti*, Russia's financial paper, that Sberbank had the right to sell its shares to GAZ if it so chose. Indeed, business daily *RBK* reported that Opel specialists had already visited the GAZ production plant, carried out an audit and test of its capacities and were happy with the result. The Russian government, in other words, clearly planned to make GAZ Opel's owner.

When, at the last minute, GM pulled out of the deal, Putin was furious, telling a cabinet meeting:

The last-minute refusal to complete the Opel deal is not harmful to our interests, but it shows that our American partners have a very original culture when dealing with counterparties. We will have to take into account this style of dealing with partners in the future. GM did not warn anyone, did not speak to anyone . . . despite all the agreements reached and documents signed. Well, I think it is a good lesson.[8]

So it's clear that there is no real dividing line between the interests of the oligarchs and the interests of the state. Most of the Russian cabinet have seats on the boards of private corporations. The state has its own oligarchs running giant state corporations and wielding immense power: men like Vladimir Yakunin, president of the state-run Russian Railways; Sergei Chemezov, head of state arms trader Rosoboronexpor; Russian Deputy Prime Minister and chairman of state oil company Rosneft; and Viktor Ivanov, who runs Russia air defence and military R&D corporation, the OJSC Almaz-Antei Air Defence Concern, as well as being the chairman of Aeroflot. Former KGB operatives feature heavily in this pantheon – companies like Alfa and Vympel Telecom are named after KGB special forces and covert assassination squads. All the oligarchs have security services run by ex-KGB agents who employ former KGB agents. As one Kremlin watcher says, 'Even Putin may be on the board of directors of Russia Inc. but it's still not clear if he can choose his own fate.'

And these are the people who are poised to buy the world. 'The Russians have spent the past few years investing in Western companies and buying up Western assets,' explains Quinn Martin at Renaissance Capital. Blavatnik, for instance, holds a 4 per cent stake in Warner Music and until recently sat on its board, his Access Industries conglomerate raised $21 billion from Goldman Sachs to fund a takeover of chemical group Lyondell in 2007, and he also owns 19 per cent of Air Berlin. Deripaska is looking for deals post-Opel. Abramovich is buying steel plants in the US. And they are also looking further afield.

'There is going to be a huge shift in capital to India and Africa where they will be competing with the Chinese for mineral resources and land,' Martin believes. 'We're just starting to see the Russians tying up huge deals in the Middle East – with plenty of Merger & Acquisition deals in the pipeline.'

The oligarchs are coming out of the recession well placed to act – a supportive state, better internal co-operation and Western banks eager to help. Their power will only increase. Indeed, they could be all over our key natural resources in the next ten years, if it wasn't for one thing: their Brazilian, Chinese and Indian rivals who might get there first. Not that there's any comfort in that – as ArcelorMittal South Africa shows.

CHAPTER THREE

IN WHICH LAKSHMI MITTAL
CLEANS UP

As you drive away from Strike Matsepo's farm, the vast slag heap on your left gives way to the factory itself, which looks like a vision drawn from Tolkien's dream of Mordor. Tall stone chimneys belch clouds of smoke, gouts of orange flame lick up into the dusk sky and a low black pall drifts across the valley.

The words to 'Jerusalem' – 'among those dark Satanic mills . . .' – keep looping through my head as I watch the desolation unroll from the back of a Ford Transit minibus driven, with a cheerful recklessness, by Bobby Peek from groundWork – a South African environmental charity that's part of the Global Action on ArcelorMittal coalition. With his Global Action colleague Sunita Dubey we're touring ArcelorMittal sites north of Johannesburg. For the last two years groundWork, and Sunita in particular, has been building Global Action into a loose network of green, trade union and human rights campaign groups from the various countries where Lakshmi Mittal – Britain's richest man, according to the *Sunday Times* Rich List 2009 and the eighth wealthiest person on the planet according to *Forbes* – has factories.

While politicians and leaders in the UK and abroad may
fête him, Global Action contends that his personal wealth of
£10 billion-plus has come through exploitation of weak local
laws and has largely been paid for by the people living near and
working in his plants. The key thing, Sunita explains, is that the
protesters are mainly from the developing world. She explains:

> It's very easy for Lakshmi Mittal to say – you know, I am
> a guy from India and the attacks are because I am not a
> northern corporate. So we had to think how to tackle it and
> how to play the racial card very carefully. We had to make
> sure it was not a northern NGO but a southern coalition
> and it should have people from India and South Africa and
> Eastern Europe. Those are the places where there are a lot
> of problems and so these are the local groups.

We turn off the blighted road and sweep into an outdoors bar
where we're meeting a bunch of workers from the sprawling
Vanderbjlpark plant for a beer. They're young men, and bulky
with the muscle of heavy physical labour. They smile but
rarely laugh and drink bottle after bottle of Redd beer. Their
view of the plant is interesting, coming as it does from the
black and mixed race children of Mandela's era. They barely
remember the early 1990s and have an only theoretical view of
life under apartheid. For them the key difference to their lives is
increasing insecurity at work and a gradual ratcheting back of
genuine corporate responsibility to be replaced by the headline-
friendly 'corporate social responsibility'. At the beginning,
they're cautious about talking – they fear for their jobs after
massive redundancies, described as retrenchments, but as the
evening passes they open up and it becomes clear that, incredibly, Lakshmi Mittal has somehow made them slightly nostalgic
for the paternalist side of apartheid.

'ISCOR [ArcelorMittal's Iron and Steel Industrial Corporation] used to have a sports ground near here,' one says, pointing vaguely into the distance. 'We had a running track, a football team, everything. They'd let you take time off work if you were training for something. But now they've sold it off, there's no team, and nowhere to train. If you do enter something, like one guy runs marathons, they'll let you take the day off if you wear an ArcelorMittal T-shirt during the race.'

'They used to give us housing, or if you rented your own place you'd get a housing allowance,' says another. 'Now you get nothing. They keep bringing in short-term workers, which dilutes the union. So the last time they made retrenchments they went through a consultation with us, but if there's anything we don't like they pretty much ignore us. We tried a strike a couple of years ago over safety but we lost . . .' He trails off despondently.

A few days before we met, a young employee had been killed at the plant. The details of what happened aren't clear but it appears that a blast furnace that had been shut down for maintenance was coming back on line and the worker – an apprentice paid for by a government training scheme – was removing the early, imperfect steel pouring out of the furnace at 1,000°C when some water from an earlier part of the process got trapped underneath. It's a critical situation in steelmaking – superheated steam trapped beneath liquid ore literally explodes, sending waves of molten metal in every direction. The worker had a full aluminized fabric protective suit covering his face, hands and body, but the heat was so intense his skin was burnt off by the trapped air as surely as if he were sitting in an oven.

The men are reluctant to talk about it, but say the government apprentices – who go through an accelerated training programme at the plant – are sometimes poorly equipped. 'There are places where you have to wear headphones specially tuned to keep the noise of the jackhammers from deafening you,' a stocky kid with a tightly shaved head explains. 'Sometimes these guys are just given earplugs. I find the noise unbearable when I'm wearing the proper headphones. How must they feel with an earplug?'

ArcelorMittal absolutely refutes this point when we meet with senior management the following day. All staff are issued with full safety equipment. There are no shortcuts. The accident was a terrible tragedy, but it was down to something going terribly wrong in a long-established procedure. As news of the man's horrific death spread through the steel industry, management assured us, other plants with the same system abandoned it and it's now been eradicated from steelmaking worldwide.

Afterwards we cram into a minibus for a tour of the old dams and drainage systems that have been leaching pollutants into the ground-water for decades. Most have been closed and there's some serious cleaning-up going on. The plant now recycles water rather than discharging it into the local rivers, and there's work underway to stabilize the vast slag heap above Strike's house. 'Just Strike left,' says Bobby as we gaze down on his tiny smallholding. 'And the ownership of that place is in question,' one of the plant managers says with a little laugh. Later Bobby picks him up on it – 'Aah, I don't know, I think I'd heard something somewhere, I can't remember,' the manager blusters. We all look away.

On the way out, we pull the Transit over to the side of the road to wait for a couple of local journalists who are following a couple of cars behind. When they catch up, we all get out and chat. One of the local reporters is interviewing Bobby and the other snapping a picture here and there, when suddenly a van with flashing lights pulls up and two burly security men jump out. 'You are still on ArcelorMittal property and I am authorized to delete every picture on your camera,' the leading goon barks, his shaven head gleaming in the afternoon sun. The journalists slip into a well-practised routine. One demonstrates the minutest details of her digital Dictaphone in case the guards could have mistaken it for a camera while the photographer conceals the evidence in the back of the Transit. The guards have a quick sniff, can't find anything, so swing into their wagon and leave.

We drive on in silence, contemplating the clean-up work. 'Do you think they're becoming the good guys?' I ask, despite being shaken by the comments on Strike's house and the cop-style physicality of the security guards. 'I don't think so,' Bobby muses.

Sunita has been listening and now leans over, speaking slowly and precisely with a soft Indian lilt:

> The thing is, in America, where Lakshmi Mittal has steel plants, you have to put all your pollution information online on a monthly basis – everything you have released into the environment, so people living nearby can see. In Europe you have health and safety laws that mean poor equipment could lead to a prosecution. Why would Lakshmi Mittal obey those laws in one part of the world and then treat his workers and the environment worse elsewhere? The Vanderbjlpark plant is the most profitable in his empire because he treats it as a developing world mill.

This global citizen began life as a poor kid from the developing world. Lakshmi Mittal was born in Sadulpur, a small, unremarkable town of some 80,000 people on the edge of the desert in Rajasthan, India. His parents were poor, with no regular income, and lived in a large house with extended family of 20 – all sleeping on rope beds and cooking in the yard.

When Lakshmi was six, his parents moved to Calcutta where his father became a working partner in British India

Rolling Mills, a small local steel company, before founding the family steel business Ispat – named after the Sanskrit word for steel. They lived in a first-floor apartment in a poor suburb overlooking some ancient tramlines. The trams would wake Lakshmi when they started rolling at five in the morning, the signal for him to get up, do his chores and walk to school. Before and after school Lakshmi would go and help his father at the mill – running errands and working in the post room.

When he was 16 he started a degree in business and accounting at St Xavier's College, a Jesuit-run school in a neo-colonial building in Calcutta. The college had a largely Christian student body and the teachers were wary about taking on a Hindu. Mittal's exam results, particularly in maths and accounting, were so good they relented but it was clear Mittal had little in common with his fellow students – they were Calcutta's golden teens. He spent the evenings working in the family business or taking extra classes.

After graduating he briefly toyed with academia, but Ispat was starting to do very well – his father had bought a large house in a wealthy suburb to the south of Calcutta and, at 21, Lakshmi was suddenly something of a catch. He met his wife Usha in a traditional way – via an arranged meeting over tea at the Calcutta Club where her mother and aunt quizzed him about his prospects. They were engaged two weeks later.

During Mittal's twenties, the steel industry was facing huge problems. Steelmaking still employed the same huge blast furnaces to produce inflexible amounts of steel as it had for almost a hundred years. They were bulky, expensive to run and expensive to build. Meanwhile demand for the product was falling around the world.

In 1975 Lakshmi's father sent him to sell some land the company had bought in Indonesia – they'd planned to build a steel mill but his father wanted to abandon the project. Lakshmi did his research and suggested a mini-mill – a new cheaper alternative to a full coking plant and blast furnace operation that used an electric arc furnace and scrap steel and which could be more quickly erected. Though an electric arc furnace produced less steel than a blast furnace in full roar, it none the less offered something unusual to a young Indian man in the mid-1970s: independence from his family.

Through a complex form of tax break, Lakshmi secured 85 per cent of the cost and equipment from the Indian government – provided he purchased everything in India. With a loan from the Bank of India in Singapore, he put together the deal, and the mill began rolling in 1977. Lakshmi and Ursa moved out to Indonesia to run the plant and it rapidly consumed all his time. Ursa, meanwhile, was raising their first son Aditya while learning the business from scratch.

In 1978 Mittal made 26,000 tonnes of steel, making a profit of $1 million on $10 million of sales. Within 11 years he'd pushed output up to 325,000 tons (330,000 tonnes). By then he had a daughter Vanisha and was 39 years old. He thought about building a second mill but then – for reasons even those who know him well are still unclear about – he changed his mind and, overnight, began his route to becoming a steel tycoon and a modern Andrew Carnegie.

Searching for scrap to feed his Indonesian smelter, Mittal came across the state-owned Iron & Steel Company of Trinidad and Tobago. It was losing $10 million per month and was managed on behalf of the government by a German company, Hamburger Stahlwerke. Mittal offered to take the plant off the government's hands and turn it around – agreeing to pay them $10 million a month on condition that, if he met every payment, he would have the chance to buy the company after five years. The government agreed.

Mittal's first cost-saving was to fire the German managers of the plant and import sharp young Indian managers whose combined salary was $18 million a year less than their German predecessors. From 1989 to 1993 the plant's output rose from 413,000 tons (420,000 tonnes) to 984,000 tons (1 million tonnes). Mittal took up the option to buy and created Ispat Caribbean.

Byron Ousey is a managing director with Gavin Anderson, a PR consultancy that specializes in advising governments and major corporations during takeover battles. He advised the Luxembourg government on its communication strategy during the ferocious ArcelorMittal takeover battle in 2006 and he co-authored *Cold Steel*, a book about that corporate contest. In the process, he met and interviewed Mittal many times. When we met in London, Ousey argued that Mittal's abrupt change of mind, when he decided not to build a second mill, but to look for opportunities for investment elsewhere instead, is the key to the man's character, and it was to be a turning point:

> After 13 years in Indonesia, he thought – it's taken me 13 years to get to 300,000 tonnes, there's no way I'm going to waste another 13 years like this. He just was so hungry. I don't think people understand that sort of hunger. It comes from the roots of being brought up on a rope bed, no running water, no electricity, trains rushing by your window, very humble. And he's incredibly focused. There's a famous story about when he took up then gave up golf. He really loved the sport and spent much of his spare time playing it. One day he was driving towards the gold course and he realized it was overtaking him. He stopped the car, turned around and went home. He never played again. That is a useful character reading of the man.

Mittal's timing couldn't have been better. For most of the twentieth century, steel had been considered a strategic resource by almost every government in the world – even the government of Trinidad and Tobago. By the time Mittal arrived in 1989, however, the islands weren't sure this policy made sense. Trinidad and Tobago's entire defence force is 4,000-strong and its air force consists of one Cessna 310 twin-engine turboprop, one Piper PA-31 Navajo and a C-26 Metroliner. If this is your army, why support a loss-making steel works as part of your strategic defence policy?

In the early 1990s, many governments were coming to the same conclusion as Trinidad and Tobago's – why lose tens of millions of dollars a month on steel plants that offer little additional security and drain the coffers of the treasury when you can sell the plants off for a quick injection of cash. In other words, Mittal had found a formula that worked and started applying it around the world.

Next came Mexico – in 1992 he bought the state-owned plant in Lazaro Cardenas. It cost him $200 million and relieved the Mexican government of a hole that was draining away $1 million every day. In 1993 he swooped on Sidbec-Dosco in Quebec. In 1995 he snapped up Hamburger Stahlwerke – home of the unsuccessful Caribbean managers – and bundled the whole lot up into a new company called Ispat International.

'His timing was perfect,' Ousey explains with a certain awed respect:

> He had fantastic support from his banks and he was [next] able to move in and buy these ageing steel plants in eastern and central Europe just as they were coming out of the Soviet era. He picked up a lot of this stuff very cheaply, regenerated the companies and turned them around to produce some very efficient plants. He bought one plant in

Poland for $100 million; it's now worth $2 billion. That's how people make serious money.

Despite these obvious successes, Mittal's family in India weren't happy. Lakshmi's father and brothers wanted to remain an Indian company and viewed this rapid international expansion with suspicion. In 1995, Mittal pulled off his most audacious deal to date in Kazakhstan, alienated his family as a result and stepped up from deal-maker to state builder in the process.

Kazakhstan was the last of the Soviet republics to declare independence in 1991. The vast land-locked state had its economy so intertwined with the centrally planned system that it struggled for years afterwards. Despite boasting the world's second largest uranium, chromium and lead reserves, as well as healthy supplies of natural gas, petrol, coal, oil and diamonds, the average salary was just $3,000 and life expectancy roughly 58.

The jewel in the crown of Kazakhstan's decrepit steel industry was the Karmet Steel works in Temirtau. It covered some 1,200 acres (486 hectares), had its own coal and iron ore mines, a power station to fire its three massive blast furnaces as well as coke ovens, rolling mills and pretty much everything needed to be a self-supporting economic entity. It was also very close to the Chinese border.

For Mittal, this was pure gold. He tried to raise the capital to buy the plant from the banks, but they were deeply suspicious of Kazakhstan and refused to lend him a penny. Instead, he began a complex and slightly opaque series of deals via a private company called the LNM Group – a company Mittal himself set up with family money and which thus had sufficient funds of its own to attract bank lending. He pulled together $400 million and bought the steel works, to the considerable relief of the reformist-minded president Nursultan Nazarbayev. So relieved was the president that he granted Mittal a complete moratorium on paying taxes and an agreement that no environmental laws would apply to the plant for ten years from the date of privatization. The Kazakh central bank was worried that a massive influx of Mittal's hard currency – to be used to cover the vast unpaid wages bill at the plant – would spark soaring inflation. Mittal chartered a plane to fly suitcases of cash into the country every 15 days. Anything to keep the deal on track.

Disputes over the Kazakhstan deal and the creation of LNM Holdings as a financial instrument within the LNM Group caused a massive rupture in the family. In the end, and against his father and brother's wishes, Lakshmi went his own way, taking Ispat International – including Trinidad and Tobago, Mexico, Canada and now Kazakhstan – and LNM Holdings with him. He combined both into LNM Group and, although Ispat was based in Rotterdam and LNM Holdings was based in the Dutch Antilles, he ran the whole empire from his new home in London. It was a complicated financial transaction that took a year to complete and the two halves of the family wouldn't speak to each other for another two years. 'I've asked him about the row many times,' Ousey says.

All he does is look down and say, 'It was very difficult.' He won't let it come out. If you look at how he grew up, at the experiences he had, and look at what close-knit families teach you, then see how he split from his family, it's a really interesting aspect of him. There are great strengths in the tight[-knit] Indian family, but a weakness as well. He got out of his country and away from the insularity of his family and began to build a vision for himself. These days he doesn't really identify himself as Indian half the time – he calls himself a global citizen.

Perhaps liberated by losing the shackles of his family business attitude, and clearly already seeing himself as a global citizen, Mittal's move to London in 1995 saw him begin spending lavishly, beginning with a house in Bishops Avenue in north London – known as Millionaire's Row for the overwrought splendour of its mini-mansions. Mittal's cost him £6 million and was grandly named the Summer Palace.

He set up the company headquarters in Berkeley Square, next to Annabel's night club, sold off 20 per cent of the company to raise $780 million and, in 1998, embarked on his most ambitious deal yet – the purchase of Chicago-based Inland Steel, a sprawling mess of a factory on the southern tip of Lake Michigan and one of the world's largest steel companies. Inland produced 18.7 million tons (19 million tonnes) a year and even though he paid $1.4 billion just as the economy teetered on the brink of recession, he was convinced he could make the kind of cost cuts that had previously secured huge profits. The deal also moved Mittal from an interesting fringe player to the heart of the world's steel industry – but it gave him a nasty shock to find the markets weren't hugely impressed. ISPAT shares slipped from a high of $28.50 to around $1.90. It gave him a suspicion of typical plc corporate structures.

Fortunately his existing plants were increasingly profitable. Kazakhstan in particular was delivering a healthy stream of cash and he used this to keep on shopping – buying mills in Algeria, Poland, Macedonia, the Czech Republic, France and Romania. With the latter, he stumbled into his first public controversy.

In 2001, the British Prime Minister Tony Blair wrote a letter to Adrian Nastase, the Romanian Prime Minister, with a very special message. 'I am delighted by the news that you are to sign the contract for the privatization of your biggest steel plant, Sidex, with the LNM Group,' the letter said. 'I am particularly pleased that it is a British company which is your partner.'[1]

When the contents of the letter were made public in 2002, questions were asked about why Blair had written on behalf of a businessman who was still an Indian citizen and had only very limited interests in Britain – indeed, during a Commons debate on the letter it became clear the LNM Group was not registered in the UK. Could the letter have anything to do with the fact that Mittal had given a £125,000 donation to the Labour Party just before the 2001 election? Absolutely not, Blair replied – dismissing the allegations as 'garbagegate' and saying that Mittal was supported because LNM was a British-*based* company, although the Prime Minister's office later conceded LNM was actually based in the Dutch Antilles and employed fewer than 100 people in the UK.

'I gave to Labour because of my love of the party and its leader,' Mittal said at the time. 'I never asked for anything, never expected anything in return.'[2] None the less, he increased his donations, gifting the party £2 million in July 2005. This cultivating of political leaders – evident from Kazakhstan to the UK – is one of Mittal's trademark moves, according to Global Action's Sunita Dubey:

When Mr Lakshmi Mittal decided to invest in India he met with Prime Minister Manmohan Singh, who then gave a public statement saying that he is so happy about this investment. At which point, all environment and building regulations become a sham because the highest member of government in the country has approved the contract. The lower-level people have to fall into place to make that happen so there is no real process. It was the same in Liberia. He goes to meet with the president and donates 100 pick-up trucks to members of the National Legislature of Liberia. They said, this is not a bribe it is just a gift. But it seems to me that there is a very thin line between bribe and gift and these dealings are at such a high level that it doesn't leave a very democratic process.

In the same year as 'garbagegate', Mittal demonstrated just how ruthless he was prepared to be in pursuit of profits. In 1996, he had paid a peppercorn fee of £11 (€1.27) for the Irish Haulbowline steel plant in Cork. In 2001 he closed the plant at a few hours' notice, leaving debts of €57 million.[3] Mittal insisted he had only agreed to run the loss-making plant for five years and could see no way of making it profitable. The Irish government was left to pay the 400 employees' redundancy money.

Mittal, meanwhile, was enjoying the fruits of his labours. In 2002 he hosted a Cuban-themed party to celebrate the 26th birthday of his son Aditya. Guests were handed Cuban cigars and gambled at specially built blackjack tables in the dining-room. In 2005 he paid £57 million for numbers 18 and 19 Kensington Palace Gardens – formerly the Russian and Egyptian embassies – and converted them into a 55,000-square foot (5,110-square metre) mansion with 12 bedrooms, a ball-room, a picture gallery, Turkish baths and a swimming pool in the basement.

In 2004, however, he topped the lot by spending a rumoured £34 million on his daughter Vanisha's wedding to Delhi-born investment banker Amit Bhatia. The proud father flew 1,000 guests to Paris, put them up in the Hotel InterContinental – three special TV channels in their rooms showed the wedding functions, movies and news – and organized five days of increasingly lavish entertainments. There was an engage-ment party at the Palace of Versailles – complete with can-can girls – followed by the ceremony at the chateau of Vaux-le-Vicomte, where Lakshmi and Usha played themselves in an hour-long re-enactment of Vanisha and Amit's love affair with a script from Bollywood writer Javed Akhtar, music by Shankar Mahadevan and choreography by dance director Farah Khan.

Bollywood stars Aishwarya Rai and Akshay Kumar performed hits from their films, Kylie Minogue belted out a few tunes, chefs flown in from Calcutta prepared a vegetarian feast of over 100 dishes while 5,000 bottles of Mouton Rothschild were emptied for a wine tab estimated at $1.5 million. After the wedding there was a disco at the Lido de Paris and opera at the Versailles Opera House. Lakshmi could afford it, though. He paid himself a £1.1 billion bonus out of company funds that year after taking over ISG, a US-based steelmaker.

'He is the new Carnegie of steel except he's not a huge philanthropist,' Ousey explains, continuing:

> He's in his late fifties, and he's not very worried about the spiritual side of things. He is a little superstitious. I saw him one day – he had a ring on his finger. I said, 'Why do you wear that ring?' He said – 'It's a sort of Indian tradition. It's not worth very much. One day I had a friend in the diamond industry who said – "You must get rid of that and get a proper ring." But as soon as I did I seemed to be dogged by bad luck. Finally I was catching a plane with my daughter and she was taken very ill. We had to rush her to hospital. I was waiting in the hospital and I took the new ring off and threw it down the toilet. Then she got better so I put this old ring back on again.'

It was in 2006 that Mittal launched his famous bid for European steel giant Arcelor – and started a vicious war of words and tactics that shook Europe's fusty boardrooms. Initially, Mittal's €18.6 billion offer for Arcelor in January was dismissed by Arcelor management and a number of European politicians, who attacked Mittal's Indian origins and the quality of his steel. Arcelor management refused to meet Mittal until a string of demands were met, while orchestrating a €13 billion White Knight deal with Severstal of Russia.

The Arcelor management suddenly gave in and negotiated with Mittal pretty much on his terms – although they did manage to force him to cede some control of his family-run company.

'He was extremely fatigued by the Arcelor battle and that shows what it took out of him because he's a very fit guy,' Ousey believes. The merger also offered an opening to the people at Global Action, who had been frustrated in their attempts to reach Lakshmi himself. The newly constituted ArcelorMittal, however, had shareholders who could be pressurized.

At the May 2008 shareholders' meeting in Luxembourg Global Action presented a document making claims about the company's extensive tax breaks, substantial borrowing of public money, as well as its cost-cutting when it came to pollution and health and safety issues. In May 2009 ArcelorMittal published a response to Global Action saying, among other things, 'many of the allegations found in the report are inaccurate and based on distorted facts'. Yet Sunita Dubey maintains:

> The company has not identified which of the facts in the report it considers to be distorted. We are committed to using accurate information, and have asked the company to give further details, however no response has been received. The problem is that I don't think ArcelorMittal can be easily embarrassed – it's not like Shell which is a long-established company with petrol stations everywhere. People can see them and connect with that. With Arcelor it's hidden. It's not out there in everyone's lives. So it's going to be a little challenging to apply pressure.

Sunita's work is only just beginning. Mittal may be the highest-profile Indian oligarch but he's by no means the most powerful or the most brutal. These days he's not even the most acquisitive. A range of high-profile buy-outs from Indian conglomerates followed the ArcelorMittal merger – such as Tata's acquisition of Jaguar Land Rover, India's United Breweries buying Whyte & Mackay whisky and London's oldest stockbroker – Hichens, Harrison & Co. – being bought by Delhi firm Religare Enterprises. Between 2006 and 2008 Indian firms made 322 deals in the US and Europe, according to research by accountancy firm KPMG, and their owners' rankings on the world's wealth lists changed accordingly.

And Indian oligarchs can operate with as much impunity as the Russian billionaires. On 2 December 2006, for instance, Ratan Tata was honoured for his 'Responsible Capitalism' by the Princess Royal in London: the company spends around $100 million a year on social welfare programmes while 10,000 of its 200,000 employees are on its various volunteering programmes. Even the company's TV commercials for its tea are a small-scale campaign against bureaucratic corruption that show small boys putting cups in front of officials on the take and saying, 'Aaj se khilana bandh, pilana shuru – Tata Tea peeyo aur kaam karo' (Drink Tata Tea and do your work).

Since 2006, however, the company has been planning and building a steel works and – to serve the plant – constructing India's largest all-weather deep water seaport at Kalinganagar in the Indian state of Orissa. Greenpeace points out that the port's proposed site is just 9.3 miles (15 kilometres) from Gahirmatha Marine Sanctuary, the world's largest mass nesting site for a rare species of migratory turtle. Every year in the six months from November to May, about 500,000 turtles congregate in Gahirmatha to mate and feed. Artificial lights from the giant port and populated areas would disorient the turtles, while pollution from the port would damage their habitat, reducing the chances of successful breeding and tipping the species towards extinction.

The plans for the steel plant in Kalinganagar, meanwhile, involve displacing at least 2,000 families – and that's just by Tata's figures. Protesters insist the number is far higher. In January 2006, hundreds of men, women and children from the Kalinganagar industrial estate arrived at the site of the plant and started a sit-in, demanding work stopped until those already evicted were adequately rehoused. Police opened fire on the protesters, killing 12 – 8 men, 3 women and 1 child – and injuring 37. Disturbingly, five corpses returned by the police after an official post mortem were mutilated; family members said one woman's breast was ripped off and a young boy's genitals mutilated, while all had the palms of their hands sliced off. It makes the two goons from ArcelorMittal South Africa seem like cuddly teddy bears.

When I got back from Africa I went for a drink with Raj, a college friend from a wealthy Delhi family, to get the measure of the Indian super-rich. I started with an account of my trip and when I wound up the story he shrugged with disdain, 'Who cares?' He leaned forward.

Listen, Mittal is nothing. He is not one of the big five families – the families like Birla who bankrolled independence. Some of those families – sure there's shit attached to Mittal but one of the other families – you know how they made it? They kidnapped one of their main rivals. That rival is nothing now; he just sits at home watching DVDs. You Brits don't know shit. Who bought the first of the Russian assets in the 1990s? Indians. The rouble and the rupee were India's only convertible currency. When the rouble crashed, the Indians froze Russian assets in India then gave them back in exchange for plants and factories on the other side of the border.

He leaned back and sighed. 'You know where I'm going this weekend? Ibiza. I'm going to party with Roman Abramovich's son. He knows the guy who runs Café Mambo. That's what's going on. No Mittals there. You think Mittal's Indian? They don't even know him in India.'

CHAPTER FOUR

IN WHICH THE TATAS GET A LICENCE
TO PRINT MONEY

Just after midnight on 3 December 1984, the Union Carbide pesticide plant in Bhopal, India, started leaking methyl isocyanate gas. Methyl isocyanate is a lethal organic compound used in the manufacture of the pesticide Sevin. Brief exposure causes coughing, chest pain and irritation to the eyes, nose and throat. Higher levels can cause lung collapse, emphysema, massive haemorrhaging, bronchial pneumonia and death.

Safety systems on the tanks the chemical was stored in hadn't worked for four years so the people sleeping in Bhopal received no warning. They woke in darkness to the sound of screams, with the gases burning their eyes, noses and mouths, retching and coughing up blood.

One survivor, Champa Devi Shukla, recalled:

> It felt like somebody had filled our bodies up with red chillies, our eyes [had] tears coming out, noses were watering, we had froth in our mouths. The coughing was so bad that people were writhing in pain. Some people just got up and ran in whatever they were wearing or even

if they were wearing nothing at all. Somebody was running this way and somebody was running that way, some people were just running in their underclothes. People were only concerned as to how they would save their lives so they just ran. Those who fell were not picked up by anybody; they just kept falling, and were trampled on by other people. People climbed and scrambled over each other to save their lives – even cows were running and trying to save their lives and crushing people as they ran.[1]

'The force of the human torrent wrenched children's hands from their parents' grasp. Families were whirled apart,' reported the Bhopal Medical Appeal in 1994, continuing:

The poison cloud was so dense and searing that people were reduced to near blindness. As they gasped for breath its effects grew ever more suffocating. The gases burned the tissues of their eyes and lungs and attacked their nervous systems. People lost control of their bodies. Urine and faeces ran down their legs. Women lost their unborn children as they ran, their wombs spontaneously opening in bloody abortion.

The best accepted estimates say that between 8,000 and 10,000 people died within the first 72 hours and another 15,000 died later. Some 120,000 have chronic medical conditions that require constant healthcare. By way of morbid comparison, the UN estimates the nuclear accident at Chernobyl caused 57 direct deaths, with a possible additional 4,000 deaths from resulting cancers.[2]

Since the accident the people of Bhopal have been campaigning for compensation, for the still-polluted factory to be cleaned up and for both Union Carbide – now owned by the Dow

Chemical Company – and its former CEO Warren Anderson to face trial. In November 2006 Ratan Tata, chairman of the family-run conglomerate, offered to pay for the area to be cleaned up. He clearly expected a warm response. What he got was furious protest – Bhopalis rounded up Tata tea bags and had dogs urinate all over them. Many suspected his offer was designed to gum up existing legal suits against the plant's owners.

Nityanand Jayaraman, a journalist and volunteer for the international campaign for justice for Bhopal, explains:

> Ratan Tata is the co-chair of US-India CEO Forum, an unofficial group of CEOs who keep suggesting new laws, or changes to existing laws to make India easier for Americans to invest in. The compensation claims always come up at the forum, and Dow keeps telling [the forum] it threatens US investment. That's why he [Tata] made the offer. He wasn't expecting the response so he withdrew it in the end. Paying to clean the area up would mean letting Union Carbide off the hook. They have to pay for the damage they caused.

There were many who seemed shocked by the Bhopalis' reaction. Ratan Tata has a solid reputation in India. He doesn't drink or smoke and his vices are limited to fast cars, jets and, at weekends, racing his speedboat across Mumbai's harbour. His bachelor pad is crammed with books, CDs and dogs. His life is clearly respectable. Indeed, just his surname is good enough for many Indians.

Neelima Chopra, scion of New Delhi society for the past 40 years, expands on this:

> During the days of the Licence Raj just after independence, Tata-Birla was really a byword for general quality. This

was a time when Indians travelling abroad would walk into shops like Selfridges, look at a handbag and be asked – 'Do you know how much that costs? I don't think you can afford it . . .'. If you went into a shop in India, most of what was on sale would be rubbish so you'd ask for the Tata-Birla stuff. It just meant the good stuff.

The Tatas belong to India's old-school super-rich. It's a family-named and -run business; indeed, despite its bewildering global expansion, the main company – Tata Sons – remains private and retains the single largest shareholding in the 27 of its 85 subsidiaries that have stock-market listings. Tata was founded in 1868 by Jamsetji Tata, a Parsee descendant of the Zoroastrians who fled persecution in Iran more than 1,000 years ago, as an opium-trading company operating out of Mumbai. It moved into hotels, steel, chemicals and power generation before the Second World War and, after Indian independence, cars and tea. Today, Tata's favourite boast is that the average Indian spends an entire day consuming its products, from the wake-up call of its Titan alarm clocks to the Tata power to light them to their beds.

When Ratan Tata took the helm in 1991, however, the company wasn't looking like a world-beater. The organization he inherited was a sprawling mish-mash of businesses involved in everything from soap to saris. Record losses at Tata Motors, a steel business that looked like a dinosaur, problems with the launch of its Indica hatchback, criminal charges over Tata Tea's alleged links with Assam militants, criticism over the sale of Tata Oil Mills' assets and a failed plan to launch a domestic airline with Singapore Airlines gave the impression that the company was struggling.

Ratan introduced a rule requiring chief executives to retire at 75, then reduced that to 65, helping him flush out some of the old guard in the operating companies. He disposed of poorly performing businesses, then set about restructuring the group.

He made the first major international acquisition by an Indian company when Tata acquired Tetley Tea in 2000; in 2007 it bought the British steelmaker Corus for £6.2 billion and in March 2008 it bought Jaguar Land Rover from Ford after workers voted for the Tata bid. The company has also made a series of lower-profile acquisitions including UK chemicals company Brunner Mond, US business General Chemical Industrial Products and the truck-making arm of South Korea's Daewoo.

Tata now owns companies operating in satellite television, mobile phones and transatlantic telephone cables; Asia's largest IT company; the world's sixth largest watch company; a jewellery company; the world's fifth largest steel company; luxury hotel chains; the world's 18th largest car company; drugs and biotech research companies; the world's second largest tea company; and even provides air-conditioning for the world's largest building, the Burj Dubai, and the world's largest passenger ship, the RMS *Queen Mary*. It's a global concern – India now represents just a quarter of the group's interests, a smaller proportion than the UK.

It's been able to expand aggressively largely thanks to the competitive advantage Tata gains from keeping the principal holding company Tata Sons in family hands. As Emily L. Walker, formerly chief of staff for emerging markets corporate banking at Citigroup, explains:

The problem Western companies have when going into a bidding war against a Russian or Indian company that's effectively privately controlled is that shareholders and local laws limit the price they can pay. The shareholder won't want to pay too much and they'll be mindful of potential scandals over low pay in the Third World or the cost of environmental clean-ups. That isn't something these [Tata] companies need to factor in.

Indeed, as the Orissa and Bhopal stories show, Tata is happy not to factor many of these things in. On the day of Ratan's 'Responsible Capitalism' award, 2 December 2006, in an obscure Singur neighbourhood in the Indian state of West Bengal, thousands of farmers and labourers were being attacked by armed police as they protested against the forced acquisition of their lands by the West Bengal government for Tata's plant to build India's 'one lakh car' (100,000 rupees – just over $2,000). Newspaper reports said that at least 80 people, including women and children, were injured.

In 2009, Tata reported deals to supply hardware and auto-mobiles to Myanmar's military junta; Tata Steel's collieries in West Bokaro and its coal washeries in Bokaro have been accused of polluting the Damodar River (http://www.american-chronicle.com/articles/view/95618); thousands of tons of boiler ash generated from Tata Steel units have been dumped in the open in the middle of Jugsalai town near Jamshedpur; Rallis India, a Tata subsidiary manufacturing pesticides, has been criticised by India's Supreme Court Monitoring Committee on Hazardous Wastes. The list goes on.

Tata has been taking some steps to clean up its mess. In 2009 the company told the state of Jharkhand that plans were in place to reclaim the Jugsalai muck heap, it (http://ecocitizen.tatasteel.com/images/mtpa-presentation.pdf) and various improvements in Bokaro have reduced air and water pollution.

It's an attitude that has echoes in the UK, where Tata employs 47,000 people. Despite initially pitching for £170 million from the UK government to bail out Jaguar Land Rover, when the cash came with conditions – government say in the number of redundancies and some sort of representation on the board of a company that was going to be spending taxpayers' money – Tata decided to raise the money from commercial banks rather than meet the government's terms. In August 2009, weeks after it refused the money, it posted a first quarter pre-tax loss of £62 million. At the time it said banking deals were close to completion, but analysts warned the financing costs could be high, forcing Jaguar Land Rover to reduce or freeze invest-ment plans for new models and potentially adding to the 3,000 redundancies the company had made since the downturn began.

On 24 September, the analysts were proved right. Jaguar Land Rover confirmed it was to close one of its UK plants – either Castle Bromwich in the West Midlands, which makes Jaguars, or its site at Solihull, which makes Range Rovers. Also in 2009, in line with pre-merger plans to cut costs by £350 million pounds, Tata Steel slashed thousands of jobs in the UK – including 1,700 in Redcar where it closed an entire plant. It was a fittingly callous end to a year which saw Tata sign a multi-million-dollar deal with the vicious dictatorship in Myanmar.

Perhaps India's economic history makes such cold indiffer-ence inevitable in any oligarch. 'Anyone who made money in the Licence Raj has a special kind of drive,' says Dr Ruth Kattumuri of the London School of Economics. 'It made them tough, it made them suspicious and it put them in a great big hurry. They always see life as, "Oh God, better not miss an opportunity." When they were growing up you didn't get a second chance.'

At Independence in 1947, the Indian National Congress Party had stripped the maharajas of their kingdoms and titles and set up a proto-capitalist economy under the new rules of what became known as Licence Raj. The rupee was not exchangeable outside India while high tariffs and a complex system of licences on imports hindered overseas goods reaching the country. An even more complex system of licences existed within India – there were around 80 different government agencies that had a say in granting licences to produce some goods. The government set prices and production quotas through a central planning policy which also dictated labour relations. The theory was that India should rely on its own internal markets to develop its economy.

The results were mixed. Up to 1990, India's GDP grew by an average of a little under 4 per cent a year. Over the same period, Indonesia grew by 6 per cent, Thailand 7 per cent, Taiwan 8 per cent and South Korea 9 per cent. In 1960, a South Korean's annual income was around four times bigger than that of an Indian, but by 1990, it was 20 times larger. At the same time, the mid-1960s saw a 'Green Revolution', led by the techno-cratic wing of the National Congress Party which had promoted new technological investment, high-yield crops and new price incentives for farmers. But in 1991, with dollar reserves too low to cover the cost of vital imports, the Indian government had had to turn to the IMF for a bailout and begin a massive programme of economic liberalization.

For some players, however – like the Birlas and Tatas – the Licence Raj worked extremely well. With only a handful of permits issued for key industries such as steel, power or com-munications, those with the right contacts could build powerful empires – and regardless of the quality of their goods, since the skills needed to start up a factory were more about greasing palms and knowing who to know than mastering production or design.

In his 1995 memoir *Inside the Steel Frame: Reminiscences and Reflections of a Former Civil Servant*, Indian MP Nitish K. Sengupta writes:

The possession of vast unregulated power in the hands of the ministers and the bureaucrats inevitably led to complaints of extortion, inducement and enormous politicization of the machinery. From 1970 supreme power was appropriated by the Cabinet Committee on Economic Co-ordination which was headed by the prime minister and for all practical purposes the prime minister's office became the main decision-making authority. No worthwhile project could be cleared without the prime minister's approval. Those who managed to get industrial licences also managed to see to it that others did not. This was done by money, influence and political muscle power. A nexus came to be established between a section of industrialists, a section of politicians and a section of bureaucrats. The principle of market forces guiding or dictating investment, or of production targets being determined by demand and supply, was given the go-by, and everything was decided by administrative fiat.[3]

It was, however, possible to play the Licence Raj system as a newcomer, as evidenced by the one of Tata's proxy business rivals, the Ambanis. Today Mukesh and Anil Ambani are India's richest and third richest men respectively – ranking 7th and 34th in the world. Mukesh heads petrochemicals giant Reliance Industries, India's largest company by market capitalization, producing oil, natural gas, petrochemicals and textiles, and also controls the retail side. Anil has the family interests in telecom, energy and financial services and, married to one-time actress Tina, has Hollywood ambitions, investing $500 million in a new studio venture with Steven Spielberg's DreamWorks as well as producing George Clooney, Jim Carrey and Julia Roberts films.

Although a vicious family feud has torn the brothers apart (more on this later, see p. 103), the combined Ambani fortune ranks fourth on the planet behind Bill Gates, Warren Buffett and Carlos Slim Helú. Their father Dhirubhai created that fortune, and his life story is a lesson in the Licence Raj game. Australian journalist Hamish McDonald captured every detail in his 1998 unauthorized biography *The Polyester Prince* – but such is the Ambanis' power that the book was banned shortly after publication.

Dhirubhai grew up in poverty, made some money in Aden in the 1950s as a teenager, then returned to India where he started working in the garment trade. The problem for India's yarn-dealers was not usually to find buyers but to secure supplies. India had one viscose factory, owned by the Birlas, and one government-owned nylon plant. These domestic factories supplied only a small fraction of local demand. Smugglers made up some of the shortfall by either misdeclaring cargoes or running small ships to the numerous creeks and beaches of India's west coast. Dhirubhai realized that the rare import licences were as good as money. By paying higher margins, he became the main player in the market for licences. The margins were tiny in the trade itself – but his dominance also put him in the position of being able to turn on and off much of the supply of yarn into the Indian market.

He set up a factory and began making his own polyester clothes under the brand name Vimal – all the while stroking senior politicians. His strongest connections were with the Gandhi clique in the National Congress Party. In 1971 they authorized a complex import-export scheme bringing in polyester and taking out nylon. Polyester was so scarce in India that the domestic price was seven times the international price, allowing the kind of price trading that Russian oil oligarchs had practised in reverse. In an interview with the magazine *Business India* in April 1980, Dhirubhai said his company, then called the Reliance Commercial Corporation, accounted for more than 60 per cent of exports under the scheme. 'The scheme was open to everyone,' he said. 'I cannot be blamed if my competitors were unenterprising or ignorant.'

Even so, Ambani lacked sufficient clout to extract the cheap government loans being doled out to better-connected businessmen. So in 1975 he incorporated Reliance Textile Industries and in October 1977 issued 2.8 million shares in the company, raising $1.8 million – one of the largest public issues in India at the time. He would use this money to foster political contacts and enter India's inner circle. Some of it helped bring Indira Gandhi back into power after she had lost an election to the Janata government of Morarji Desi. Ironically, it was used to bribe MPs to swap sides during an inquiry into government corruption. Dhirubhai also paid for Indira's welcome-back party at the Asoka Hotel in New Delhi, where she spent two hours receiving well-wishers with him at her side.

It was a savvy move. In 1979, when Indira returned to power, Ambani's company barely made it to the list of India's 50 biggest. By 1984, Reliance was in the top five. Dhirubhai also had an easy time from the Finance Ministry. For years Reliance paid no corporate income tax on its profits, becoming the most famous of India's 'zero-tax' companies. 'It is not for nothing that this dark horse from Gujarat has achieved the reputation in textile circles of being the best friend and the worst enemy one could have,' according to *Business India* in May 1985.

Dhirubhai spent the early 1980s as a shirtsleeves populist – holding shareholder meetings in packed football stadiums and personally taking on and breaking short-selling cartels (traders selling shares in the company that they didn't have and gambling that the share price would fall far enough for them to pick up the necessary shares at a cheaper price than their initial deal) looking to dump his share price. He worked in an expensive office in Bombay's Nariman Point business district, drove around in a Cadillac and had his own helicopter, but he still played the part of the outsider. Rumours abounded that he handsomely rewarded those financial journalists who helped maintain that image.

In 1985 the accession of ex-pilot and clean pair of hands Rajiv Gandhi broke Dhirubhai's political connections. An investigation into tax evasion and fraudulent letters of credit prompted India's now defunct Mumbai tabloid *Blitz* to worry that 'the conclusion becomes inescapable that, since 1969, a single industrialist had been literally dictating the government's textile and import policies and manoeuvring import rules to "kill" his rivals and maintain his lead in the market'.[4] Dhirubhai worked hard to bring Rajiv around and by the end of the decade had official permission to build a plastics plant and a natural gas refinery – both of which reduced costs for his vast polyester industry. He also bought several newspapers. In November 1988, the entire Ambani clan moved into a company-owned 17-storey apartment building with car parking, a gymnasium, a swimming pool and several floors of guestrooms.

In 1989, however, Mumbai police arrested a senior Reliance employee Kirti Vrijlal Ambani (originally Kirti Shah, but he changed his name to impress his boss) and charged him with conspiracy to murder Nusil Wadia, who ran Reliance's biggest rival, Bombay Dyeing. Reliance has described the charges as 'preposterous' and has disassociated itself from Kirti's actions. The national Central Bureau of Investigation moved to take over the case, but this prompted a reporter on the *Indian Express* to discover the son of the CBI's director Mohan Katre was on Dhirubhai's payroll, and the case drifted into touch. In 2001, *Business Week* commented that Kirti was still awaiting trial.

By the middle of 1991, India's economy was in trouble. There were insufficient dollars to pay for imports, New York credit rating agencies lowered their rate for Indian sovereign debt, Iraq's invasion of Kuwait sharply pushed up India's oil import bill, and some 3 million Indian workers had to be evacuated from the Gulf at government expense. Anger at the IMF's emergency loan – and the assassination of Rajiv Gandhi by a suicide bomber – returned the National Congress Party to power. Under Prime Minister Narasimha Rao and Finance Minister Manmohan Singh India globalized.

Although the favours of Licence Raj ended, the Ambanis prospered. Investment banks flocking to the new India found Dhirubhai was someone they could do business with. In February 1994, Rao's cabinet awarded three oil and gas discoveries in the Arabian Sea to a consortium involving Reliance, Enron and the government's Oil and Natural Gas Corporation, which had discovered the fields but didn't have the funds to develop them. Reliance entered the oil-refining business, grabbing a quarter of the domestic market, and won licences to operate a basic telephone service in Gujarat as well as various mobile phone licences covering nearly one-third of the Indian population. It even managed to survive a massive stock-exchange scandal in 1996–97 by paying a fine that *Business Standard* described, in October 1996, as 'a tap on the wrist'.

'Today the fact is that Ambani is bigger than government,' a lawyer told Hamish McDonald in the late 1990s, explaining:

> He can make or break prime ministers. In the United States you can build up a super-corporation but the political system is still bigger than you. In India the system is weak. If the stock exchange dares to expose Ambani, he tells it: I will pull my company shares out and make you collapse. I am bigger than your exchange. If the newspapers criticize, he can point out they are dependent on his advertising and he has his journalists in every one of their departments. If the political parties take a stand against him, he has his men in every party who can pull down or embarrass the leaders. He is a threat to the system. Today he is undefeatable.[5]

Dhirubhai's sons still rule the roost though, having taken over the business when the old man died in 2002 without leaving a will. Both have flamboyant lifestyles. Anil has a playboy past, Hollywood connections and makes repeated attempts to buy into English Premier League clubs. Mukesh bought his wife a Boeing jet as a birthday present, while construction of his 27-storey Mumbai home will cost an estimated $2 billion and boast its own cinema, swimming pool and helicopter pad.

Indeed, they are technically the richest family in the world – although their fortunes may never be combined. The two fell out in 2004 over the terms of Dhirubhai's will but agreed to divide Reliance in a settlement brokered by their mother. Since then, however, the sniping has been constant. In 2008 Mukesh foiled Anil's attempt to buy South African mobile phone giant MTN. Today their communication is through lawyers, PR firms and pleasantries at family breakfasts with their mother, Kokilaben.

The feud regularly dominates the front pages of Indian newspapers. When, in April 2009, an engineer found mud and stones in the gearbox of Anil's helicopter – which would have caused a fatal accident if not spotted – conspiracy theorists went crazy. Whoever placed the pebbles in the engine understood helicopters, Anil's pilot R.N. Joshi said in a police statement. The chopper would have been able to take off but the debris would have entered the gear box and cut the power, bringing down the aircraft. In May, the dead body of the engineer who discovered the debris, Bharat Borge, was discovered on a suburban Mumbai railway track after a train hit him. According to various newspaper reports, two employees of the aircraft maintenance firm were arrested for the sabotage, the police specifically ruling out business rivalry and saying the incident appears to be connected to a union dispute; while the police initially thought that the engineer's death was a suicide, but later said they believed it to be a tragic accident.

The recession hit both brothers, but a rebound in the Indian stock market – which by October 2009 had more than doubled from its lowest point in early March – means those losses are being clawed back. New oil refineries coming online, a major oil find off India's east coast and one of the world's largest discoveries of natural gas beginning production in April 2009 certainly helped. In *Business India*'s 'highest earning' chart, published in November 2009, Anil emerged as the highest-paid man in India.

Indeed, as the *Business India* chart shows, post-recession the Indian super-rich seem fine. In September 2009 the Altamont investment fund – which deals with individuals able to invest $15 million or more – announced it had signed up seven Indian investors and expected to have a further 15 on board by the end of the year.

Certainly the country that was a sleepy place for the world's wealthiest now has a fast-rising stock market, a booming real estate sector and rich-friendly tax laws – notably the 2004 elimination of capital gains tax on the sale of equity, bought in a boom which saw the beginning of change. By 2008, there were 53 billionaires in the country, slipping to 24 in 2009.

The new rich aren't shy about flaunting their wealth. Flamboyant liquor tycoon Vijay Mallya counts a fleet of vintage cars, a stud farm with 200 racehorses and a castle in Scotland among his personal toys. Despite recent financial troubles, he paid $1.8 million at a New York auction in 2009 to buy Mahatma Gandhi memorabilia. Then there's Naresh Goyal, who founded and runs Jet Airways, India's leading domestic airline, with his stucco-fronted townhouse overlooking Regent's Park in London and a Mumbai villa stuffed with his huge art collection, or telecoms magnate Bhupendra Kumar Modi, who has a home in Beverly Hills as well as three in Singapore – buying a new $10 million penthouse apartment in the city in May 2009.

In New Delhi these days you can find Prada and Pearls Parties – where the biggest pearls and flashiest handbags win the day; or Carat Parties in Mumbai which, according to one party girl, are basically private events where women are allowed in only if they have a ring of high enough carat value. 'It's a way of organizing a social scene for the wealthy based purely on money, rather than the trappings of class left over from years ago – which might see impoverished ex-military officers holding memberships for clubs that used to be the preserve of the elite,' insider Neelima Chopra explains.

Private yachts bob off the coast of Mumbai and Goa while private jets scream into airports in luxury destinations or urban business districts. New Delhi's DLF Emporio Mall, which opened in 2008, has consistently defied the downturn, launching a new designer brand store almost every day. It now hosts some 74 international designers – including Burberry, Dior, Gucci, Versace and Marc Jacobs – and 111 Indian designers and has plans for further upmarket shopping malls in Mumbai, Chennai, Hyderabad, Kolkata, Ludhiana, Chandigarh, Ahmedabad and Pune. BMWs and Jaguars stream past on roads once populated entirely by clunky Ambassador cars, a version of the pre-Independence Morris Oxford.

The Indian rich are a truly global elite, although London remains the billionaire's first choice. They fly in for opening weekends of exhibitions at the Victoria & Albert Museum, or head to Dubai for the Cartier Polo. Children of the new rich studying in London will have a flat, a Porsche and a chef – because they're unlikely to have cooked a meal in their lives. Eurotrash dives like Palm Beach Casino, Cipriani's and Nobu are rammed with Indian millionaires, rubbing shoulders with newly minted Russian and European wealth.

To some extent, of course, India's super-rich have been in the job far longer than those in the other BRIC countries. In the days of the British Empire, the maharajas had the wealth, land, palaces and staff of any European royal family and brands like Cartier and Louis Vuitton had a proud presence selling to these regional rulers who had been co-opted by the British to keep order in their provinces. Indeed, Cartier himself personally designed jewellery for the wedding of the Maharaja of Kapurthala almost a century ago. Some Indians are used to luxury.

Yet, in the same week Altamont declared its new investors, farmers in the Punjabi village of Veeralapalam were struggling with drought after a poor monsoon season. Many of the lower-caste farmers have no access to irrigation wells sunk into the lava bedrock by wealthier high-caste farmers. A few could buy a dousing of costly piped water from a nearby creek, although most cotton and lentil farmers were preparing for the long trip to Hyderabad where they would have to work as rickshaw drivers to pay off their debts. Around 450 million Indians live off rain-fed agriculture, with the monsoon providing 80 per cent of their precious water. With almost half of India's 604 districts affected by drought, August saw at least 20 farmers commit suicide, so parlous is the outlook. Indeed, for the vast majority of India's population, it is still a daily struggle to have enough to eat and get clean drinking water.

In September 2008, Raghuram Rajan, Professor of Finance at the University of Chicago, former chief economist of the IMF and head of the Committee on Financial Sector Reforms in India, told the Mumbai Chamber of Commerce and Industry that India was not equipped to help its poor:

> Ration shops do not supply what is due, even if one has a ration card, teachers do not show up at schools to teach, the police do not register crimes, or encroachments, especially by the rich and powerful, public hospitals are not staffed, public sector banks do not want to lend.

At the same time, he said, when comparing billionaires to a nation's GDP – how many super-rich individuals a country has compared to its overall wealth – India runs Russia a close second:

> Three factors – land, natural resources and government contracts – are the predominant sources of the wealth of our billionaires. And all of these factors come from the government . . . too many people have gotten too rich based on their proximity to the government. Corruption in India's political establishment used to be about the sale of permits during the Licence-Permit Raj. Reforms have created new sources . . . Scarce national resources like forests, coal, and minerals can be allocated. Land can be expropriated from those who do not have connections or formal title, converted to industrial use and allocated. Public land can always be disposed of to favored parties. Contracts can be assigned to chosen friends despite a sham of public bidding. If Russia is an oligarchy, how long can we resist calling India one?[6]

And India's oligarchs have soaring international ambitions. Tata has identified eight countries for expansion – the United States, the UK, Singapore, South Africa, the United Arab Emirates, South Korea, China and Bangladesh. As befits a company with a long history of greasing up politicians – even today the Tatas are among the largest contributors to both the National Congress Party and the Hindu nationalist BJP – it's doing so with more than a few favours from government. In September 2009 Tata secured £10 million from the UK government to help it develop an electric car despite the company's insistence that it will close factories, adding to the hundreds of job losses at its steel works and car factories.

November 2009 saw Mukesh Ambani's Reliance Industries pick up where it left off pre-slump – buying up stricken US petrochemicals group LyondellBasell, which has large UK plants in Milton Keynes and Carrington. These oligarchs are heading west – not to escape a change in government but to buy up steel, cars, chemicals and natural resources. Their skills were forged in a corrupt economy. They do deals with dictators but win awards for corporate social responsibility.

How long will it be before all of us begin our day drinking Tata tea or coffee for breakfast, wear clothes bought from Westside shopping centres, take a Tata car or bus to work, where we use a computer set up by Tata Consultancy Services, lunch in a Tata hotel, and use Tata power to light our homes – and will that power be generated in plants built on the severed hands and mutilated breasts of those who protest?

CHAPTER FIVE

IN WHICH THE PRINCELINGS IGNORE THE PAUPERS

On 31 September 2009, the Chinese Revolution threw its 60th birthday party – although, this being China, the public was largely excluded and local residents were warned not to stand on their balconies for fear of arrest. Above the Gate of Heavenly Peace in Tiananmen Square, President Hu Jintao watched from the spot where Mao Zedong had announced the establishment of the People's Republic in 1949. He smiled and waved as mechanized weapons systems trundled past – unmanned aircraft, tanks and missiles, most of them appearing for the first time in public. As each went by, the official commentator marvelled at how they had all been developed in China.

They were followed by a fly-past of 150 military planes and helicopters, then Zhai Zhigang, the first Chinese 'taikonaut' to walk in space, waving from a mock-up of his Shenzhou 7 spacecraft. The air force even claimed the blue sky was down to the biggest weather modification project in history – dispersing two days of thick Beijing haze to let the sunshine in. The point of the display was to demonstrate how modern the socialist state had become, so there were fewer soldiers than usual – barely 8,000.

But the parade had something of a twentieth-century feel all the same – indeed, at times it had the old communist kitsch of the Cold War era. Schoolchildren flipped over coloured cards to create slogans reading 'loyalty to the party', and 'harmonious society'. Various groups of ethnic dancers shrugged off recent political unrest by jiving past the viewing stands. There were even displays based on petrochemical installations and new railway engines. The technology might be new, but in essence China's approach seemed unchanged. In 60 years the country appeared to have come a long way while staying exactly on the same spot.

Beneath the surface of such huge state events, however, the rise of China's super-rich can be found. At the 2008 Olympics in Beijing, for instance, Chinese billionaires were as crucial as the Communist Party in building and supporting the event. Hotel chain Century Golden Resources Group, run by billionaire Huang Rulun; sportswear chain Li Ning, owned by the eponymous Chinese gymnast who won gold at the 1984 Los Angeles Olympics, and Beijing property developers Zhang Xin and Pan Shiyi were among many others to help supply the games. The so-called 'Green Games' also relied on a batch of Chinese billionaires leading the world in green technology – from solar water heaters through energy-efficient light bulbs to wind turbines.

To find them, anyone keen to know what the real future of China will be – the country that overtook Japan in 2009 to become the world's second largest economy – should have tip-toed away from the march past and caught a newly privatized plane to Shenzhen, the city right next door to Hong Kong. Set up as a Special Economic Zone in 1980 by Deng Xiaoping, the city has grown from a tiny village with barely 30,000 inhabitants to a multi-billion-dollar export machine, helped on by the Chinese government allowing it a number of firsts – first stock exchange, first shopping mall, first McDonald's.[1]

The average Shenzhener is 27, and carving out a place in the world with stupefying success. In June 2007, 20 per cent of China's PhD graduates lived and worked in the city. Stepping over the border from Hong Kong, the seasoned Asian traveller comes face to face with endless BMWs and Audi TTs (they like their cars German in Shenzhen), all bought in via Hong Kong with ruinous import tariffs. Such is the wealth in the city, however, that the rate of cars coming over the border only seems to increase. In China they have a saying: 'You think you're brave until you go to Manchuria, you think you're well-read until you reach Beijing and you think you're rich until you set foot in Shenzhen.'

The city is the home of China's wealthiest man – Wang Chuanfu – and his electric car company BYD, as well as Zhang Yin, the country's richest woman, and China's most generous philanthropist Yu Panglin. China's oligarchy is more subtle and complicated than post-Soviet Russia. China stepped carefully when embarking on its privatization programme and the Communist Party seems to vacillate between embracing the market and renationalizing. This, of course, does not prevent a very small group of people making an enormous amount of money and wielding an almost medieval level of power. In modern China there are two ways to join this group – as an insider with good Party connections or as an outsider who takes a chance.

Wang, for instance, is the latter. BYD's current HQ is a silvery office building with golden pillars framing the entrance. The sprawling complex looks freshly plucked from Silicon Valley. Despite the utilitarian furniture, conference tables groan under plates of fresh fruit. But Wang – 43, slim, with black hair and glasses – grew up in extreme poverty in rural

China. His parents, both farmers, died before he started school. His brother and sister supported him until he was old enough to take the long train ride from the village to Central South Industrial University of Technology, where he earned his chemistry degree. In 1990 he completed a Master's at the Beijing General Research Institute for Nonferrous Metals and settled into a quiet life as a government researcher – trying to make better batteries.

Frustrated by the lack of funding available to government researchers, Wang borrowed $300,000 from his relatives and set up on his own making nickel batteries in 1995. He called the company Build Your Dream – a name that caused sniggering when he started exhibiting at motor shows in the West. These days he often jokes that it means Bring Your Dollars.

BYD had so little capital that Wang couldn't afford to import an automated battery production line from Japan. Instead he used semi-automated equipment that he had pieced together from technical manuals. He took extreme advantage of China's low labour costs, substituting migrant workers for machines. In place of the robotic arms used on Japanese assembly lines, which cost $100,000 or more apiece, BYD hired hundreds, then thousands, of people to assemble products at a price Sony and Sanyo struggled to beat. They responded with a barrage of lawsuits, all ultimately settled out of court.

Thirteen years later, BYD is the world's largest producer of mobile phone batteries – with 30 per cent of the market – and the second largest producer of rechargeable batteries for laptop computers. The biggest story, however – and the reason that Warren Buffett took 10 per cent of BYD at the start of 2009 – was Wang's move into the car market. BYD's F3 car is the most popular domestic car in China, but Buffett was betting on the E3 and the E6 – two fully electric family cars launched in 2009. Electric cars are expensive to make, and the single largest cost is the battery, but Wang claims to have designed a breakthrough low-cost version that makes a mass-market electric car possible. To prove it, and to illustrate how harmless his patented fuel cell was, footage of him drinking the electrolyte from it was posted online.

Such stunts are unusual. In the rare moments he's not at the office, Wang lives in a modest penthouse flat with his wife and daughter. He spurns the obvious trappings of the very wealthy, like corporate jets and expensive clothes, but he does own three Mercedes and a Lexus, which he likes to tell interviewers he owns because he enjoys taking them apart to figure out how they work. This lack of conspicuous consumption seems at odds with the rest of the world's wealthy – surely the richest man in China can splash out on a nice house? – but in China's complex oligarchy, it doesn't do for an outsider to stand out.

There are two Rich Lists in China – *Forbes* and the *Hurun Wealth Report*, published independently by Rupert Hoogewerf, the journalist who created *Forbes*' first Chinese list over ten years ago. Both are taken equally seriously by the wealthy – for reasons good and bad. The *Financial Times* Beijing correspondent Jamil Anderlini explains that both lists have a nickname in China – the Death List:

> Since *Forbes* first published a China Rich List in 1999, names like Sichuanese tycoon Mou Qizhong, actress Liu Xiaoqing, orchid king Yang Bin, Shanghai developer Zhou Zhengyi, entrepreneur Tang Wanxin and investment boss Zhang Rongkun have been jailed for crimes from tax evasion through fraud to bribery.

In 2009 Chinese novelist Wang Gong published *The Curse of Forbes*, about Feng Shi, a wealthy misanthrope, who falls for an unspoiled beauty named Jiang Qing, but despairs as he knows his days are numbered. '*Forbes* is a curse, you know,' Feng explains. 'If you get on to the list you'll be dead meat in no time.' In a review of the book, *Forbes* asked whether 'anyone in China is safe from the curse'?

Hoogewerf traced the stories of the 1,300-odd people who have featured in his list and found two awaiting trial, ten under investigation, seven who had been investigated but not convicted, seven who had fled China, and six who had died (including two suicides and one murder). There are 18 in jail, including Zhou Zhengyi, 11th richest in 2002, who heads up the Nongkai Group, and was sentenced to 16 years in 2007 for bribery, embezzlement and tax fraud; Zhang Rongkun, 16th richest in 2005 and the owner of Fuxi Investment, who was sentenced to 19 years for his role in a billion-dollar pension fund scandal in Shanghai; and Zhou Yiming, 207th richest in 2005 and chairman of Shenzhen Minglun, which has businesses involved in electronics, trade and food processing, who was given a term of life imprisonment in April 2007 for contract fraud. Though less than 2 per cent of the names on the list, it's still an intriguing statistic.[2]

Anderlini comments:

Everyone is suspicious of the super-rich, and there's this phrase bandied about: 'original sin'. The words in this context seem to have originated with a Communist propaganda official called Feng Lun, who, ironically, has since gone into the property business. He suggested a few years ago that any early entrepreneur must necessarily have made his 'first bucket of gold' through shady transactions, since China's legal system was so restrictive it was impossible to get rich otherwise. It basically means loans that were never repaid, land that was acquired by dubious means or state assets that were stolen.

One *Hurun Wealth Report* Rich List rags-to-riches story in the classic Dick Whittington tradition illustrates the risks some billionaires face. Behind-the-scenes machinations can mean that any bold young fortune-seeker is as likely to have his cat torn to shreds by a swarm of bloodstained rats as earn eternal riches and glory. Wang's predecessor at the top of the list in 2008, for example, followed a fairy-tale arc to a less than happy ending.

Huang Guangyu, sometimes known by his Cantonese name Wong Kwong-yu, grew up in Shantou, a poor district in southern China's Guangdong – the area that used to be known as Canton. As a boy, he recycled bottles after school to supplement the income of his farming family. At 16, with his elder brother Huang Junqin, he headed north to Mongolia, where he sold cheap watches by the side of the road before moving to Beijing and setting up a street stall selling radios and gadgets bought cheap from factories near his home town.

He moved into his first shop with his brother in 1987 and beat off the competition by delaying supplier payments and cutting profit margins, earning him the nickname 'price butcher'. In 1992 he split the stores and the property business with his brother – taking the shops himself and relaunching them under the brand name Gome, China's first private retail chain.

His 'original sin' was a line of credit from the Bank of China, secured to help expand. The loan was given when the bank was happily lending – so not exactly a theft of state assets. When he married a bank official working in the loans department, however, official eyebrows were raised. In 2004 he listed Gome on the Hong Kong stock exchange and embarked on an amazing buying spree, snapping up shops and chain stores across China and introducing the country to the concept of the hostile takeover.

Huang's office was presidential, complete with an en-suite bedroom for overnight working sessions, and he was chauffeur-driven between meetings in a stretch Mercedes. In interviews, however, he liked to insist that his personal tastes were frugal, pointing out that he, his wife and three children still lived in a cheap apartment rather than splashing out on a fancy address. He gained coverage in the style press for shaving his head – possibly to indicate an ascetic, monkish attitude – but spoiled the effect by arriving at parties in full tux and bald nape.

In 2006 rumours swept power circles in China that Huang was under investigation for dubious bank loans worth 1.3 billion yuan (around £120 million). He was investigated, along with his brother, but both were released and cleared of any charges in January 2007. Word had it that Huang had strong military connections and had asked them to 'disappear' the problem, but these were allegations that were never proved. If so, it proved a bad move. People far, far higher up than his protectors resented this Get Out of Jail card and when Huang appeared at the top of *Forbes* and then *Hurun Wealth Report*'s China Rich Lists in 2007 and 2008, the curse struck.

On 19 November 2008, aged 39, Huang disappeared. Business magazine *Caijing* reported that police had taken him in for questioning over accusations he'd manipulated share trading in two listed companies, Sanlian Commercial Co. and Beijing Centergate Technologies Co. His wife had been put under house arrest. After that, silence . . . filled with frenzied business press speculation. Huang had attempted suicide, he was selling his stake to JPMorgan, he would be tried, then he wouldn't be tried. He resigned as chairman of Gome in January 2009 and faced charges in the autumn. Hurun's 2009 list still featured him – based on his current assets and ability to trade in shares even from prison. He'd lost his place at the top spot, however, to 43-year-old Wang Chuanfu with $5.1 billion.

'People certainly attract more attention once they get listed,' Ren Jianming, dean of the anti-corruption research centre at

Tsinghua University in Beijing, told *The Times*. 'Maybe other rich people who aren't on the list also did business in ways that probably did not comply with the laws, but they may get less attention.'[3]

Despite the threat, the *Hurun Wealth Report* estimates that Beijing is home to 143,000 dollar millionaires, Shanghai has 116,000, Hangzhou around 42,300, Chengdu some 12,200 and Shenyang 6,900. Although Shenzhen can claim only 40,000 millionaires, most of the rest owe their fortunes to its favour. When Deng licensed the city's Special Economic Zone, he wasn't sure if China would get its hands on Hong Kong, so decided to experiment with capitalism in a highly restricted environment. He picked the original Shenzhen village – with a population of 30,000 – and drew up a plan that allowed for expansion to a total zone of 116 square miles (300 square kilometres). The city council calculated that the population of the city would have grown to 300,000 after five years and set about structuring their building and public works programmes accordingly.

In the real world, however, the young and ambitious flocked to Shenzhen in such numbers that the figure was three times that. After fresh plans failed, the council abandoned its predictive modelling in the second half of the 1990s and mounted a fire-fighting urban planning style, attempting to provide for the 8 million official residents and at least as many unofficial residents as best they could. Thus the vice-president of urban planning in Shenzhen, Xu Chongguang, is keen on imaginative architecture that can be put together quickly and realizes that it's his priority to impose order on the wildfire, ugly-as-sin expansion of the last thirty years and introduce parks and public spaces into Shenzhen's packed urban sprawl.

Then, in January 1992 – 12 years after founding the zone – Deng Xiaoping found himself facing his own Yeltsin moment, and it was to Shenzhen that he turned for support. Fourteen years previously, in September 1978, with the help of a small cadre of likeminded thinkers, the previously marginalized bureaucrat had effectively taken control of the Chinese Communist Party at the Third Session of the Eleventh Party Congress.

It was three years after Mao Zedong's death, and the country – as well as the Party – had been struggling to recover from his grim legacy. The economy was at best stagnant, while neighbouring Japan, Hong Kong, Taiwan and Singapore were growing at incredible rates. Mao's successor Hua Guofeng had arrested the Gang of Four, the clique around Mao that started the savage bloodshed of the Cultural Revolution, but seemed to have no clear ideas and even less support when it came to planning the future.

Deng's vision was to switch the central plank of the Communists' ideological economic structure from Hua's favoured collectivization and industrialization to a broad-based economic modernization – including a tacit acceptance of the end of collective farming and the rights of farmers to operate as separate economic units. In rural areas, the household contract responsibility system began to spread across the country after trials in Fengyang County saw the amount of food its farmers sold to the government in the first year of the new system equal the entire total for the previous 26 years.

The slow move to the market began. Under a system of small collectives known as Town and Village Enterprises (TVEs), a kind of community capitalism broke out, overseen and technically owned by local government officials. So-called 'red hat' entrepreneurs, who hid their ambitions behind Party loyalty, used TVEs to shelter their schemes from Party investigation. For instance, the first Chinese company to be quoted on NASDAQ in 2002, Qiaoxing Group, began life in 1992 as a TVE in Fujian, with its founder Wu Ruilin using the front of a government-owned business to spend the capital he had accumulated in the garment trade developing the telecoms giant.

Deng also began freeing up prices – gradually removing the vast differential between global market prices and the heavily subsidized Communist prices. Eventually the difference between internal and external prices would allow Russian oligarchs to make their fortunes, trading state assets with the outside world. Although this wouldn't happen in what was still the Soviet Union for another five or ten years, the potential problem was clearly something that worried Deng. He began a slow easing of the state controls known as the Ten Regulations. In effect, these allowed certain groups to sell any surplus left over from the government's central plan at prices as much as 20 per cent above or below the set price. By 1985, the prices of 40 per cent of farm products and 34 per cent of consumer goods were completely free of government regulation.

In 1988, Deng decided to go further faster and introduced a sudden relaxation of prices. Inflation rose sharply – one of the grievances that provoked the Tiananmen Square protests – and bouts of civil unrest alarmed the Party old guard. Conservatives froze the reform programme, imposed martial law and renewed official hostility to private companies. In a sense, it was the tanks outside the Kremlin moment – but unlike Russia, which had just seen Gorbachev's resignation, Deng the reformer prevailed.

In 1992, at the height of the Party's internal dispute, Deng took a holiday in Shenzhen. This was a move that must have warned the conservatives he was up to something. There are, essentially, five interesting things to do in Shenzhen: eat, shop, head out to the beach at Yantian and revel in the tropical heat without being put off by the vast decommissioned Soviet aircraft carrier that's moored offshore, get drunk – or make a vast adjustment to China's internal politics with a barnstorming speech. Deng chose the latter.

He began his 'southern tour', a self-conscious reference to Mao's own policy tours, with a speech on socialism and capitalism:

> The reason our reform and opening are slow in pace is we're afraid of becoming capitalist. It is a matter of choosing between socialism and capitalism. We should judge by the standards whether it can develop socialist productive forces, enhance the comprehensive power of socialist countries and improve people's living standards.[4]

Reform might mean a little 'spiritual pollution' of communist values, but whenever you open a window you let in flies. He accused his opponents of being like women with bound feet – the phrase being another little loan from Mao. He said that China should open itself to foreign investment – private capital served the cause of development as well as education and scientific research. China would have to accept, he added, that in a race for riches, some people would emerge as winners long before others.

And he was right. Hurun's 2009 *Wealth Report* shows a country that seems to have barely brushed the recession as it passed on its way to global domination. China's rich spent 2008–09 getting richer. The cut-off point for making the top 1,000 richest Chinese rose from $100 million in 2008 to $150 million in 2009. The number of US dollar billionaires, meanwhile, reached 130, up from 101 in 2008. *Hurun Wealth Report* publisher Hoogewerf believes there to be at least the same number again that he has not yet found.

And there are plenty more on the way. In 2008, China over-took the UK in the number of its millionaires, according to a survey by Merrill Lynch and Capgemini. The two firms expect millionaires in the Asia-Pacific region to outnumber those in the US by 2013, mainly thanks to China.

In 2009, Hoogewerf outlined the Chinese millionaires' life-styles in a report on the so-called 'new aristocrats', based on extensive interviews in six cities. The typical 'new aristocrat', he wrote, is in his forties, lives in Shanghai with his wife, and has a son about 17 years old who's probably studying in the UK.

> He owns a villa in the city and an apartment in Beijing, has four cars in his garage, enjoys playing golf, has paid more than $515,000 to join golf clubs and sometimes he and his friends will charter a plane to play golf in Hainan province. He has four watches including a Vacheron Constantin and an Oyster Perpetual Datejust, and his wedding ring is very likely from Tiffany Legacy. He has recently developed a liking for wines. Chateau Lafite Rothschild, costing about $34,000 per crate, can be found in his cellar, and he smokes Davidoff Classic No 2.[5]

In August 2009, *China's Luxury Goods*, a report from brand marketing agencies Ruder Finn Inc. and Albatross Global Solutions, compared a general decline in demand for luxury brands in Europe, America and Japan, with the booming Chinese market. According to the report, 2008 saw China over-take the US to become the world's second largest luxury goods market after Japan – accounting for 25 per cent of global sales. China's Ministry of Commerce predicted the country would become the world's largest luxury market by 2014.

Beijing now glitters with luxury malls – with security guards to keep the riff-raff out of course. There's Seasons Place Mall, in Xicheng district, which has the usual suspects – Calvin Klein, Louis Vuitton, Chloe, Agnès B. etc. – as well as Lane Crawford, mainland China's first branch of Hong Kong's legendary luxury department store. With 2008 sales growth on the mainland at

42 per cent, Gucci opened three new stores in Wuhan, Shanghai and Beijing over the summer of 2009 and its shoe designer Salvatore Ferragamo announced that the company will open eight new stores in Chinese malls in 2010.

Browsing through Seasons Place in summer 2009 was 43-year-old Lucy Li, who runs her own import–export company from Dalian City in north-east China's Liaoning Province, from which she makes several million yuan (several hundred thousand dollars) every year. That day she was buying her 20th luxury watch – a Patek Philippe – for $8,000. Li said she spent around $30,000 on suits, shoes and watches the previous year:

> I'm very confident that my income will increase and I think it's important to have these things. It makes me comfortable and confident wearing them. And if some of my friends who earn about the same salary as me can buy Louis Vuitton bags, then I should be able to buy one too.

Insane and extravagant purchases by mysterious wealthy figures are becoming commonplace. In September 2009, for instance, the *Tibet Sun* reported that a woman – who would only give her name as Wang – paid $600,000 for a Tibetan Mastiff in north-west China, then flew it back to her home city Xi'an in northern China, where a convoy of 30 black Mercedes-Benz picked her and the dog up at the airport.

Chinese artist Zhang Huan prefers to draw attention to a different lifestyle. In the autumn of 2009 he was invited to direct Handel's opera *Semele* at La Monnaie in Brussels and used a 450-year-old Ming dynasty temple as the centrepiece of his production. He explains how he came on it and the story it unveiled, leaning forward over a low table and smoking throughout our conversation:

About two or three years ago when I went to acquire this temple there was someone still living there. They didn't really want to sell, but they needed the money to build a more modern house to allow the son to find a good wife and start his life. With an old house he wouldn't be able to find a good wife. In China there are strict government rules about taking down structures like this so it had to be done in secret. We had to go to the house, dismantle it and bring the structure back to the studio. With the house I acquired a lot of the owner's possessions – everything from socks and shoes to clothing and books. I found a diary kept by the man – now dead – who had shared the house.

The diary was his record of his love and hatred for his wife and his helplessness in the face of the poverty that they lived in. They were in the country. The jobs were not well paid and they had no money. So he wrote about the tragedy surrounding the family. He was an alcoholic. He drank because his wife had an extra-marital affair. She would leave the house and not come back for a month or two. That was the relationship – he'd get drunk, beat her, she'd leave, come back a month later, they'd fight, he'd hit her, and it would start again. As soon as she had left he would regret being a bad husband and want to see her but he would feel this anger and hatred for his wife and her lover. It got so he couldn't take it any more and so one day he and a friend conspired to hire a man to kill her lover. The job was done. They had him killed. But it is not possible to get away with this. So then he was arrested and executed by a firing-squad.

He twists his mouth and stubs out his last cigarette. 'You know, I think this is more common in China that you might believe. For most of the people life here can be very hard.'

This refrain is picked up by one of the architects of Deng's reforms, an economist called Wu Jinglian – a man so influential his ideas formed the thinking of a generation of economists in senior government posts, including Zhou Xiaochuan, the leader of China's central bank, and Lou Jiwei, chairman of the country's vast sovereign wealth fund. A child of rich intellectuals who ran a newspaper in Nanjing, Wu fled the Japanese advance, joined the Communist Party and during the Cultural Revolution was thrown into the countryside, where he was regularly beaten for being anti-Maoist and an effete intellectual. After Mao's death his reforming star rose and fell until Deng's 'southern tour' moved him into government, where he acted as adviser to Premier Zhu Rongji and President Jiang Zemin. His aim was to blend the market with his socialist ideals – taking a softer line than Russia's Anatoly Chubais – and his role in China's growth is seen as crucial.

In a series of interviews around China's 60th anniversary in October 2009, however, Wu sounded unhappy. 'Education, medical and health work and other rudimentary public services still fall short of people's expectations,' he told the *International Herald Tribune*, identifying a widening income gap and inefficient monopolies, and complaining that corrupt officials and business tycoons had hijacked the economy and manipulated it for their own ends. The system, he warned, had become a form of crony capitalism.

Certainly success or failure as a 'red hat' capitalist is all about relationships. In 2006, for instance, two little-known private companies paid just under $550 million for a vast industrial conglomerate called Luneng, valued at more than $10 billion. State regulators had received no notice of the sale – usually a legal requirement – and a tangle of overlapping boards and shareholders obscured the owner's identity. Nearly half the money used to buy Luneng was untraceable. When the Chinese business magazine *Caijing* reported on the details of the deal, the authorities removed the story from the magazine's website and cleared the magazine from the news-stands. The magazine's staff were convinced the story came close to implicating the children of senior Party leaders – still a huge taboo.

When President Hu Jintao granted Namibia around $250 million in loans in 2007, meanwhile, it seemed merely convenient that some $55 million should go to Nuctech – a Chinese firm run by Hu's son – to provide cargo security scanners. When the Namibian government started investigating a bribery scheme in early 2009 that suggested Nuctech had given kickbacks to secure the deal, Chinese government censors blocked internet surfers from searching for news about the younger Mr Hu, Namibia or Nuctech.

These sons and daughters are the Princelings, the children of senior Party officials. According to one experienced China hand, the country is effectively run by some 100 to 200 families who 'see the state as their property and the state's assets as their personal fiefdoms. They operate above the law – they're effectively untouchable.'

In August 2009, *Time Weekly* – a Chinese magazine – cited a joint project between several senior government research bodies that claimed 91 per cent of the 3,220 people in China worth over 100 million yuan (£8.75 million) were 'children of senior cadres'. *Time Weekly* quoted Cai Jiming, a member of the standing committee of the Chinese Communist Party Political Consultative Conference, saying that 0.4 per cent of China's population controls 70 per cent of the country's wealth. The story caused a huge online buzz and *The People's Daily*, the Chinese-language mouthpiece of the Party, published a quick and comprehensive rebuttal of the claims, insisting that Cai hadn't given any such quote.

However, Chen Weihua, a columnist for *China Daily* – the country's official English-language newspaper – largely accepted the story. 'While some have challenged the data's accuracy,' he wrote around that time, 'it is hardly a secret that many people have used the official power and influence of their parents and relatives to rake in some big bucks in a short time.'

Many of these Princelings went into business as the country started to open up, grabbing positions at the top of large state-owned enterprises controlling much of the country's resources. The son of current premier Wen Jiabao is CEO of Unihub Global Network, a large Chinese networking company. The daughter of former premier Li Peng, Li Xiaolin, is chairman of China Power International Development Ltd, an electricity monopoly, and Li's son, Li Xiaopeng, was chairman of state-founded Huaneng Power International, the country's largest independent power company, until his promotion to Deputy Governor of Shanxi Province.

Li Peng's Princelings are particularly unpopular examples. Li Peng himself was already notorious by the time of their fall from grace: he was prime minister of China during the Tiananmen Square demonstrations and took full responsibility for sending the tanks in, and also drove through China's Three Gorges Dam project, since blamed for vast environmental devastation and the displacement of almost 2 million people. Li Peng was behind the deregulation and privatization of the power industry so it's at least curious that his family ended up in control of large parts of it.

Li Peng's successor Zhu Rongji was equally fortunate in his offspring. Zhu, who stepped down in 2003, shaped the nation's economic policies for almost two decades. A former mayor of Shanghai and governor of China's central bank, he oversaw the country's entry into the World Trade Organization in 2001 and approved international share sales by state-owned companies.

His son Levin Zhu went from government weather analyst to investment banking via a remarkable circuitous route. After studying at Nanjing Institute of Meteorology in eastern China from 1977 to 1981, he spent two years in Beijing analysing global weather patterns at the China Meteorological Administration. He then moved to the US, where he was awarded a doctorate from the University of Wisconsin-Madison with a thesis on the study of the Indian Ocean sea surface temperature on the large-scale Asian summer monsoon and the hydrological cycle.

In 1996, Zhu received a Master's degree in accounting and joined Credit Suisse First Boston in New York. Two years later, the year his father became premier, Zhu joined China International Capital Corporation, a three-year-old investment bank set up by Morgan Stanley, the Government of Singapore Investment Corporation and Hong Kong tycoon Payson Cha. Having forged personal ties with state-owned companies to win underwriting assignments from China Life Insurance Company and China Petroleum and Chemical Corporation (known as PetroChina), Asia's largest oil refiner, Zhu went on to wrest control of the bank from Morgan Stanley in a long war of attrition.

Although his connections may have helped him secure and retain control, as well as secure PetroChina's $2.9 billion stock market flotation in 2000, they didn't help his company's performance after Daddy left office. In 2008 China International Capital Corporation earned 90 per cent less than its rival Citic Securities Co. It lost market share in stock underwriting, its biggest source of fees, and fell behind in trading. Zhu now faces competition from Goldman Sachs Group Inc. and UBS AG, the first Wall Street firms awarded licences to manage share sales in China.[6]

Morgan Stanley is trying to sell its stake, but that hasn't stopped investment banks cosying up to the Princelings. 'They [China's leading politicians] all send their children to do an internship in a Western merchant bank,' says the *Financial Times*' Jamil Anderlini. 'There are people whose job it is to ID the Princelings and get them an internship in their bank. If you go round one of these banks you'll see a group of Chinese kids all sitting together – they're the Princelings.'

Today, the 'red hat' capitalists and the Princelings are advancing together. Take Huawei (pronounced Hwa-Way), a fast-growing, privately owned Chinese producer of routers and switches – devices that act as 'bridges' or 'translators' for text or information between networks. Founded by a former People's Liberation Army officer, Ren Zhengfei, the Shenzhen-based firm posted £4.5 billion in sales in 2008. The company is now the world's number-two equipment supplier to the mobile phone industry – just behind Ericsson, having over-taken Alcatel-Lucent and Nokia-Siemens in 2009 according to Dell'Oro, a research firm in California.

And Huawei is still growing: earnings are up by 42 per cent a year as it isn't afraid of touting for work anywhere it can, even in the most war-torn regions of Africa. After winning a pitch it sets up camp, quite literally, around its client, providing tempo-rary homes for thousands of Chinese engineers. Once there, Huawei involves itself in all aspects of the developing world nation's cultural life – indeed, it recently shelled out to sponsor Zimbabwe's national football team.

Ren, a sprightly 65-year-old worth around $120 million, likes to model himself on Chairman Mao – spouting folk witti-cisms, purging associates and challenging US power. He credits Mao's guerrilla warfare strategy as a guide for Huawei's 'bat-tles' with multinational companies – inspired by Mao's ideas of 'occupying the countryside first in order to encircle the cities' he targets markets in small cities and remote areas where multinational giants rarely bother to establish a presence.[7] Like Mao, he likes to cloak himself in mystery. The details of his biography are sketchy, although everyone from the CIA and MI6 through to his commercial rivals is keen to unpick the details.

Ren was born in 1944 during the Japanese occupation, and his father fled to Guangdong to work in the KMT party's arms factory as an accounts clerk, then, when the war was over, became a headmaster. With scholars and intellectuals coming under attack during the Cultural Revolution, Ren's father was a target during the purges of the 1950s. In a rare interview Ren recalled that his father had once wished for death but wouldn't commit suicide for the sake of his seven children.[8] He was beaten and mocked on an almost daily basis for years, and warned his children to be very careful whom they trusted.

Ren attended Chongqing University of Civil Engineering and Architecture, then joined the army, working as an engineering director for the Chinese military's telecom research department in a unit based in Sichuan. This is where he built up significant contacts in one of the country's most powerful market players – the army. 'When Procter & Gamble launched in China they found the only organization that could get their products to every city was the PLA [People's Liberation Army],' says Cheng Li, a senior fellow at the John L. Thornton China Center of the Brookings Institution. 'Its network of commercial interests was very important in China until 2000.'

With the Cultural Revolution still hanging over China in the 1970s, his family was regularly denied access to schools and hospitals, even when seriously ill. His mother suffered from TB and Ren travelled across China to find medicines for her, meeting civilian Party bosses to add to his military network.

When he lost his job after the research department was downsized in 1978, Ren spent a few years unemployed, then moved to Shenzhen, where he started Huawei in a shabby, one-room workshop as a low-cost alternative to big-name firms like Cisco and Ericsson. In 1988, Huawei began providing communication technology to the Chinese military, a deal that Ren's extensive contacts helped secure. The firm also supplied Saddam Hussein with an illicit communications system in 2000, according to the CIA, and has been accused by Cisco of stealing designs for routers.

All of this helped Huawei to become, in just over two decades, the world's third largest maker of mobile telecommunications gear, with 40,000 employees, 10,000 based outside China, and research facilities in Plano, Silicon Valley, Stockholm, Moscow and Bangalore, India, along with six laboratories in China. In Europe, Huawei supplies Vodafone, Deutsche Telecom, France Telecom and Telefonica. Foreign orders now account for 75 per cent of its $18.3 billion turnover.

Ren's military ties and Huawei's refusal to reveal its ownership structure are starting to cause concern, however. In January 2007, after a joint venture between Huawei and US telecoms company Nortel collapsed, the Rand Corporation produced a report for the US air force that warned, 'Huawei maintains deep ties with the Chinese military, which serves a multifaceted role as an important customer as well as Huawei's political patron and research and development partner.'[9] A month later, the conservative think tank the Heritage Foundation issued its own report, arguing that Huawei was a threat to national security and warning that 'if a PLA protégé firm acquired an American firm that provided computer network equipment, software and services to the US government, the possibilities for cyber-espionage would be virtually unlimited'.[10]

A $200 million deal with India's Reliance Communications in 2007 survived these security fears, but a bid for a minority share of US-based computer network maker 3Com in 2008 did not. The White House's Committee on Foreign Investment blocked the purchase over fears that the Chinese military would gain access to 3Com's cybersecurity unit, known as Tipping Point, which sells software to the US military.

Meanwhile, in March 2009, British intelligence warned that equipment installed by Huawei as part of a new BT communications network could be used to halt critical services such as power, food and water supplies. A briefing document on cyber warfare worried that, while BT had taken steps to reduce the risk of attacks by hackers or organized crime, 'We believe that the mitigating measures are not effective against deliberate attack by China'.[11] In July, the Australian Security Intelligence Organisation began a similar investigation, clearly alarmed by the idea that a powerfully connected billionaire with contacts at the highest level of the Chinese military and political establishment had installed key elements of the nation's communications grid – terrified at the idea of 'red hat' and Princeling, hand in hand.

It's a fear the world's raddled car industry was in no position to resist after China swept through the West on a corporate shopping spree in 2009. After the Shanghai Automotive Industrial Corporation and Nanjing Automotive Corporation divvied up MG Rover's assets between them in 2005, then merged in 2007, the country, um, hit the accelerator. Privately owned Geely, based in the eastern province of Zhejiang, surprised the industry in 2006 by unveiling a small, sleek, silver sedan at the Detroit Auto Show. The company has several joint ventures, including one with Manganese Bronze, manufacturer of the iconic London black cab. In 2009, Geely offered to buy Volvo from Ford, launching a series of attempted acquisitions: Sweden-based high-performance sports car maker Koenigsegg Group

AB sold a significant stake to Beijing Automotive Industry Holding Corporation, allowing them to bid for Saab, and heavy machinery maker Sichuan Tengzhong bought Hummer.

It's not just cars. The past year has seen Chinese state and privately owned companies buy US and European investment banks, Canadian oil and mining companies, Japanese technology firms, Middle Eastern petrol corporations, Australian iron, copper and gold mines, swathes of mineral-rich land in Africa, natural gas in Iran, American computer giants and South American oil assets.

In early February 2009, for instance, Zhongjin – China's third largest zinc producer – bought a controlling stake in Perilya, a medium-sized zinc and lead producer in Australia. The following week, Hunan Valin Iron & Steel picked up a 16.5 per cent stake in Fortescue, Australia's third largest iron ore producer, for $771 million while Sinosteel bought nearly 6 per cent of iron ore mining company Murchison as well as its closest rival Midwest Metal Products.

Over the summer, China Investment Corporation bought 1 per cent of Diageo, the world's largest drinks company; 17.2 per cent of mining giant Teck – which owns a significant chunk of Canada's oil; swathes of commercial property in the US, UK and Australia, from office buildings to shops and hotels; stakes in Hollywood film productions; expressed interest in LVMH Moet Hennessy Louis Vuitton; and paid out for chunks of the financial sector with stakes in JPMorgan, Blackstone and commodities trader Noble Group.

The country's thirst for oil lead Sinopec to buy Addax Petroleum, which operates an oil field in Iraq's Kurdistan region; PetroChina to buy into Singapore Petroleum Co. and Japan's Nippon Oil; while Sinochem Group, China's fourth largest company, bought UK-based Emerald Energy, which owns oil and gas in Columbia and Syria, for $875 million.

'China clearly sees a promising opportunity in the raw materials field in which it can benefit from its cash pile at a time when companies abroad need money or asset prices are cheap,' explains Jonathan Fenby, director of China Research at Trusted Sources.

Bloomberg analyst Matthew Lynn agrees:

> The Chinese want control of raw materials. Take Africa – the Chinese are very heavily involved in Africa because it's a mess and China is a very big powerful place. In Angola, there's an £800 million deal to develop a new oil field, Sudan sells some two-thirds of its oil to Beijing and the country has spent another £1.2 billion on a new off-shore oil field in Nigeria. Meanwhile, Beijing has acquired mines in Zambia, textile factories in Lesotho, railways in Uganda, timber in the Central African Republic and retail developments in almost every capital. It's a bit like the British in India in the eighteenth century. The colonization of Africa is a possibility.

So deeply interwoven are the Princelings and the super-rich that holding out against a rapacious Chinese takeover can bring the full force of the state down on your head. In June 2009 China was infuriated when Rio Tinto, an Anglo-Australian mining giant, walked away from an offer by Chinalco, an aluminium firm, to double its stake in the firm. Instead, Rio struck a deal with BHP Billiton, its largest competitor. In July the Chinese police arrested Stern Hu, an Australian who heads Rio's iron ore operations in China, and three of his colleagues. Initially accused of stealing state secrets to strengthen Rio's hand in iron ore pricing negotiations, Hu was eventually charged with the lesser offence of commercial espionage and taking bribes.

'Everyone's suspicion is quite understandable,' says one oilman with experience of both Russia and China, before continuing:

> In my experience the Chinese probably have some reason for the arrest. They play a slightly straighter bat than the Russians. If the Russians were pissed off with you, you'd be better off getting out of the country like the BP guys. Even so, there's very little you can do if they've decided you've acted against their interests in some way except hope it passes.

This hunger for natural resources is potentially alarming – and helps explain China's desire to keep Australia close, funding Australian MP research trips and buying up Australian securities to help Prime Minister Kevin Rudd's bailout.[12] Where the country already has a monopoly, it has started to wield the power that brings. For instance, it now accounts for 93 per cent of the production of rare earth elements and 99 per cent of three in particular: neodymium, dysprosium and terbium. Rare earth elements tend to be at the heavier end of the periodic table and, although far more common than the name suggests, are hard to find in sufficient concentrations to make mining them economically viable.

Dysprosium and neodymium are soft metals that react easily with oxygen and can be highly magnetized at low temperatures. As a result they are used to make the very light magnets essential in the manufacture of wind turbines and hybrid engines. The Toyota Prius, for instance, uses a couple of pounds (roughly a kilogramme) of neodymium in each engine.

A single mine in Baotou in Inner Mongolia produces half of the world's rare earth elements. Most of the rest comes from small private and sometimes unlicensed mines in southern

China run by 'red hats'. For the past three years, China has been reducing export quotas and, in a secret memo, in summer 2009 outlined its six-year plan for rare earth production, a plan which, according to leaks, will see it applying further annual limits. The plan also requires Western companies to move factories to China instead of buying the elements for import. Ultimately, the green energy industry will have to do whatever China says.

Which brings us back to Shenzhen, Wang and Warren Buffett. The idea of a cheap, mass-produced electric car is clearly wonderful. But, as recent history shows, Wang is already a target simply through his wealth. Those that co-operate with the Princelings survive. Those that don't disappear, and the state takes the company anyway. In a few years' time, Buffett may find himself, like Robert Dudley, on the sharp end of a Chinese version of the TNK-BP débâcle. The examples are apposite. The Russians have the oil, the Chinese have the green technology and the West can do . . . well, what?

CHAPTER SIX

IN WHICH LULA DOES THE HULA FOR THE MOOLAH

In the constant ferocious competition for top spot as São Paulo's most luxurious boutique, Daslu walks away with the title every single year. Set in a landscaped park in the city's affluent business district Vila Olimpia, the $50 million, four-storey neo-classical palazzo boasts two gardens, two function rooms that can be converted into cinemas, theatres, catwalks or concert halls at the touch of a button and a café with spectacular views of São Paulo. The 30 in-store outlets are staffed by sales assistants with their own personal assistants, all dressed in little black dresses with white lace collars and cuffs, who fetch tired shoppers an espresso while they check out more than 60 designer labels, home décor, flatscreen TVs, cars and – should anyone be in the market – aircraft. Anything and everything is for sale.

Lucia Piva de Albuquerque founded Daslu back in 1958 in a small boutique at the heart of the upmarket Vila Nova Conceição district but it was her daughter Eliana Tranchesi who decided to expand it in the early 1990s, in the midst of Brazil's terrifying financial crisis. She set off on a charm offensive bringing Christian Dior, Dolce & Gabbana, Prada and Gucci to her store and positioning everything perfectly for the boom that followed.

By 2004, Daslu had outgrown Vila Nova Conceição and began the move to the Vila Olimpia palace of consumption. At the vast rooftop shindig that marked the new store's opening in May 2005, 2,000 of Brazil's most beautiful enjoyed an all-day festival of eating, drinking, dancing and shopping, finishing up with an all-night party on the roof terrace. Daslu's owner Eliana drifted elegantly through the crowds with her long blonde hair and trademark black dress explaining the glory of the new Daslu: 'You could buy a new Jaguar, a penthouse by the sea or a helicopter if you want and we guarantee to have everything delivered to your hotel in under three hours.' A helicopter? I was, obviously, stunned. 'Yes,' she smiled. 'After all, we didn't put a heliport on the top of the building just because it sounded like a funny idea.'

There is, of course, another reason for the heliport. A significant number of Daslu's clients choose to arrive at the store by chopper because the heavily guarded building nestles between a highway and the sprawling favela, or urban slum, Coliseu. Arriving by car – even an increasingly common armoured car – is tempting both fate and armed gangs.

Most of Brazil's wealthy seek safety through stealth. They only descend from their armoured vehicles in guarded garages. Indeed Brazil's armouring industry – including some 120 companies – is a world leader. It had its first big break in 1999, when bandits tried to kidnap the children of banker Jorge Paulo Lemann. Breathless reporters described how the bandits' bullets bounced off his armoured car's windows.

Even the car rental company Maxiauto has 30 armoured vehicles on offer. BSS Blindagens, another São Paulo company, has an armoured Smart minicar in its showroom. As it weighs just 1,700 pounds (771 kilogrammes) with a mere 85 horse-power (*c.* 1,275 cc), it may be the world's smallest passenger vehicle capable of resisting a .44 Magnum.

Given the unfortunate juxtaposition of shop and shantytown, it's no surprise that Daslu has become a symbol of extravagant consumption in a country with one of the world's widest income gaps. In 2008, Brazil's GDP was the world's ninth largest at almost $2 billion, just behind France at $2.1 billion and the UK at $2.2 billion,[1] but a quarter of its population – some 40 million people – survive on less than $2 a day.[2]

At the opening party Tranchesi insisted she was well aware of Brazil's social problems but was doing her part by providing jobs, paying taxes and giving free day care and schooling for her employees' children. And, she pointed out, her armed guards and gated compound were far from exceptional in the country. Rio de Janeiro's luxury gated development Jardim Pernambuco alone houses 140 millionaires' mansions on a hill-side high above the city.

That didn't persuade Davida, an HIV charity that works with and is largely run by Brazilian prostitutes. As a form of protest and revenue-earner combined, Davida created the idea of a fashion line called Daspu after Brazil turned down $40 million in US aid in 2005 because American law required the nation to sign an anti-prostitution pledge. Daspu is a double gag – an abbreviation of '*das putas*', or 'from the whores', and a play on Daslu's position and prestige, mocking the store's power and geography. Eliana threatened to sue but things started to slip for her and a more pressing court case demanded her attention.

In July 2005, shortly after the Vila Olimpa store opened, 300 armed police and customs agents raided the store and its offices. They arrested Eliana and her brother Antonio, claiming they were about to burn documents that proved their complicity in a vast smuggling and tax evasion scam. According to police,

Tranchesi and other Daslu employees evaded at least $10 million in taxes by using fake companies abroad to under-report the value of its imports. Later that year nearly $1 million worth of Chanel and Gucci bags were confiscated at Guarulhos airport. On 13 December 2006, Daslu was fined $112 million for tax evasion. In March 2009, brother and sister were convicted of smuggling, organized crime and tax evasion. Eliana was sentenced to 94 years in prison.

And this is part of Brazil's internal conflict. On the one hand things look beautiful. The country is the world's leading exporter of ethanol as a bio-fuel, with half its cars running on pure alcohol. Already self-sufficient in petrol, it discovered massive offshore oil fields in 2007. According to Moody's Investors Service – which raised the country's sovereign debt ratings to investment grade in autumn 2009 – Brazil's economy barely dipped during the recession. 'Evidence of strong economic and financial resilience ... can be seen in the modest and short-lived contraction in GDP, minimal weakening in the country's international reserve position, moderate deterioration in the government debt indicators and lack of financial stress in the banking system,' according to Moody's assessment.[3] By 2050, Brazil will have the fourth largest economy in the world.

On the other hand, this wealth is unlikely to help Davida's charges. Instead it's creating the world's newest oligarch class – with the same aggressive past and global ambitions as their Russian, Indian and Chinese colleagues. In their June 2009 report Merrill Lynch and Capgemini put Brazil third after India and China in terms of creating the greatest number of millionaires in recent years. The number of Brazilians worth more than $1 million jumped almost 20 per cent, giving the nation more millionaires than both Australia and Spain and putting it 10th in the report's global millionaires chart.[4]

The newly minted wealthy are cashing in on a boom in commodities from soybeans to iron ore – Brazil is the world's largest exporter of coffee, sugar, chickens, beef and orange juice, and ships vast quantities of soya, iron ore and wood pulp. Billionaires like mining magnate João Carlos Cavalcanti; industrialist Antônio Ermírio de Moraes, chairman of Votorantim Group, which produces metals, papers, cement and electricity, and Joseph Safra, who runs Safra Group, a banking and investment conglomerate, are climbing rapidly up the ranks of the super-rich. They, like Brazil, had a good recession. *Forbes* estimates their fortunes rose by hundreds of millions of dollars over 2009.

Brazilian international expansion may not be treated with the same reverence as that of the other three BRIC countries, but it's starting to become noticed. In May 2009, a vast loan from the government bank BNDES helped enable Brazil Foods – already the world's biggest chicken processing and export company and with a 90 per cent share of Brazil's pasta market as well as huge pork and beef sales – to expand its enterprises. It has targeted the Middle East for its next step – with Brazil's centre-left president, Luiz Inácio 'Lula' da Silva's help. His relationship-building at diplomatic levels filters down into business deals. It's safe to assume Brazil Foods will do well. People start eating lots of meat when they reach an income of about $10,000 per person and 80 per cent of the world's population have yet to reach that point. Piggybacking on Brazil's developing world contacts, Brazil Foods will be there when they do.

Meanwhile, in 2008, InBev, a Brazilian brewing giant that already owned Europe's largest brewer, spent $52 billion buying America's Anheuser-Busch to become the world's largest brewer. Carlos Brito, the Brazilian chief executive of InBev, who now oversees Stella Artois, Beck's, Budweiser, Hoegaarden and Brahma, may be rising up the ranks of the super-rich but he's largely considered the public face of the real power – Jorge Paulo Lemann. Based in Switzerland since the attempted kidnap of his children in 1999, the billionaire Brazilian financier is leading an aggressive global acquisition charge. He moved from banking to beer in 1989 and ruthlessly pursues savage cost-cutting with every new purchase. Buying Anheuser-Busch lead to $1 billion in savings, mainly achieved by abandoning the worker-friendly policies of the American beer giant and laying off 1,400 employees at Budweiser's home town of St Louis.

Is this a pattern when fun-loving, samba-inventing Brazilians buy Western companies? Ask the nickel and copper miners of Sudbury in Canada. Around 1.8 billion years ago a 6.2-mile (10-kilometre) meteor hit the earth pretty much where the town of Sudbury now sits. As a result, the area is unbelievably rich in minerals, boasting one of the world's largest supplies of nickel and copper ores. There have been mines there for over 120 years – which is pretty much the only reason anyone would live in the bleak, remote town – and the Canadian company that ran the mines, Inco, provided 32 per cent of the world's nickel.

In 2006 Companhia Vale do Rio Doce, known as Vale, the Brazilian mining conglomerate, bought Inco. Vale immediately began moving its equipment suppliers – choosing overseas ones rather than local. The company also began preparing to take on the powerful Canadian mining union that organized in Sudbury.

Greg Baiden used to run R&D for Inco:

> The ore body in Sudbury is huge. . . . People are going to be mining it 600 years from now. In mining, however, you have three factors – the resource, the reserve and your costs. The resource is the amount of material that can be mined. The reserve is the percentage of that you can mine at a profit. Your costs make the difference between the two.

In Sudbury, 65 per cent of your costs are labour. The unions have built up safety, wages and bonus structures that are very expensive. When I was running R&D, my job was to develop the next generation of technology that would bring these costs down. We wanted to use machinery almost exclusively when it came to the actual below ground mining, keeping the employees on the surface. This would have increased productivity and kept the deaths per tonne low – which is the only safety metric that can really apply across time. We had two choices: to take on the unions or to gradually let people retire, leaving their jobs with dignity and respect after helping to build the company up over years, and let the new generation work with the new tech. I preferred the latter. Unfortunately Vale preferred the former.

Baiden believes Vale decided to break the Canadian union when Sudbury's union leaders invited union officials from Vale mines and plants across the world – Madagascar to Brazil – to a conference at the town's Steelworkers Hall to discuss globalized unions:

At that point Vale decided – no way. The problem for the union guys is that the world has changed and they didn't notice. Sudbury is a tiny part of Vale's global business. They've got warehouses packed with nickel that they're withholding from the market to keep prices high. They can just let that trickle on to the market and park the whole town. The union guys can't hold out anywhere near as long as they can.

In July 2009, over two-thirds of the company's employees at its Sudbury factory walked out after a contract dispute. Vale started forcing non-striking engineers, managers and admin workers off desk jobs and into the mines. By November, the strike had cost the town over $20 million, forcing local business to close down.

When we spoke in December 2009, Greg Baiden was deeply pessimistic and expected the strike to become violent:

> I walked into a restaurant the other day and there was this table of young miners, and as I walked past you could hear their talk and hear the tension. A few days later I'm at a football game and there's an older guy behind me rah-rahing the union – I wanted to say to him, do you remember what it's like being 28 with two kids and a car loan? We're weeks away from the coldest part of the year. Some of those young guys are going to cross the line and all hell's going to break loose. The town is going to tear itself apart.

Vale chief executive Roger Agnelli insists that 'Sudbury is the company's highest-cost operation and isn't sustainable at current price levels.'[5] Vale has even threatened that the company's Canadian business is in jeopardy.

It all seems so brutal compared to the soft, warm fuzzy feeling generated by Brazil's president. Lula came to power in 2003 promising to haul millions of his compatriots out of poverty, and he has moved a little in that direction. More obviously, however, his tenure has coincided with an unprecedented boom for the rich. Lula currently enjoys a historic high approval rating of 57 per cent among Brazil's wealthiest citizens.

In fact, specific government-backed projects have benefited a number of billionaires with tight, oligarch-style links to the government. In September 2009, for instance, the International Olympic Committee capped the year by awarding Rio the 2016 Olympics – the first time a South American city will host the event – and oligarchs were intimately involved, financing the bid and preparing for lucrative contracts in the wake of its success.

One of them, Brazil's richest man, Eike Batista, donated 23 million reals ($12.9 million) to the campaign – about a quarter of the bid's entire budget – and gave Lula his private jet to fly to and from Copenhagen. This wasn't entirely self-less. Batista's EBX Group runs mining, energy, logistics, oil and gas, renewables and entertainment conglomerates, while Batista himself owns hotels and resorts. He stands to do very well out of large-scale construction programmes.

'If the Pan American Games are any indication, some of the Olympic contracts will be offered without a public tender,' says one Western oilman based in São Paulo. 'It stinks, but it happened. The cynic would say that it could happen again and people like Eike who backed the bid enthusiastically would then be in a good position to benefit.'

According to journalist and author Chris McGowan, who lives in Rio, the Olympics are 'a coming-of-age ceremony for Brazil as a budding superpower, much as the 2008 Beijing Games were for China', but he warns that Brazil's endemic corruption could wreck the whole event:

> Brazilians would be far better off, and the country a vastly different place, if they refused to tolerate the rogues' gallery that populates their federal, state, and city governments. The Congress in Brasília is known for a total lack of ethics, lavish benefits for senators and deputies; secret votes; shameless appointing of family members to federal jobs; and ingenious diversions of money for personal or political ends. Lula's political allies have been tainted by one corruption scandal after another since he was first elected. Yet, nothing much sticks; charges are dismissed

or never followed up; and no guilty career politician gets more than a slap on the wrist, no matter how extreme the vote-buying or money laundering.[6]

If anything, the corruption appears to be getting worse. When the Committee to Protect Journalists issued its 2009 list of countries where journalists' lives are in peril and freedom of the press is threatened, Brazil was the sole newcomer among the 14 named. Although Brazilian authorities have managed to prosecute some journalists' murders, many more have barely been investigated, and successful prosecutions have not reduced the nation's high rate of deadly violence against the press. And those journalists not threatened may still have their voices muzzled if they dare to take on the wealthy and influential.

In July 2009, for instance, Judge Dácio Vieira of the Federal District Court in Brasília banned the Brazilian daily *O Estado de S. Paulo* and its website Estadão.com from publishing reports on a corruption scandal involving the former Brazilian President José Sarney – a scion of the country's old money super-rich and currently chairman of the Brazilian Senate. Judge Vieira announced that *O Estado de S. Paulo* would be fined 150,000 reals ($82,400) for every story published on the case – and extended the punishment to all Brazilian news outlets that reproduced the paper's stories.

The censorship seems vengeful – indeed the paper appealed the decision on the basis that Judge Vieira is a close friend of the Sarney family. It also seems pointless. *O Estado de S. Paulo* was the first newspaper to report on Sarney's nepotistic awarding of federal contracts – essentially handing them out to his relatives and close friends – as well as his misappropriation of funds and tax evasion, but the story has since run across the world. Known in Brazil as 'Operação Faktor', or 'Boi Barrica' – a reference to a legendary monster from the

State of Maranhão where Sarney's family and power base reside – the story was based on transcripts of recorded telephone conversations between members of the Sarney family during a police investigation centred on Sarney's son Fernando, who is accused of a range of financial crimes including money laundering.

The *Estado*'s allegations – and this comes from a conservative newspaper rather than a radical campaigning organ – include the mysterious disappearance of 500,000 reals ($260,000) of the 1.3 million reals ($746,269) that a foundation bearing Sarney's name received from the state oil giant Petrobras. These funds somehow passed into various front companies and ultimately the pockets of Sarney's family. At the same time, some 70 so-called 'secret Acts' by the Brazilian senate passed between 1995 and 2009 directly benefited Sarney and numerous family members and associates were employed in lucrative no-show jobs at the Senate.

Sarney defended himself in an impassioned and lengthy speech to the Senate in August. He denied even knowing one beneficiary of a Senate job, Rodrigo Cruz. Newspapers then published pictures of Mr Sarney at Mr Cruz's wedding, next to the happy couple. New claims were still emerging in the autumn and Sarney denies them all.

Sarney first ran for office half a century ago and for the past 40 years he has controlled the fortunes of Maranhão, on the eastern fringe of the Amazon. It's a backward region. Many people live in single-room houses roofed with palm fronds, lacking running water and electricity. Infant mortality is 60 per cent higher than the national average. The centre of São Luís, the state capital, is decrepit – streets are pitted with potholes and gangs of unemployed residents hang around pitching for tips in return for showing drivers where to park. The murder rate is high even for Brazil.

Sarney has represented this region as federal deputy, governor and senator. In 1985 he accidentally became the president of the entire country when the man chosen for the job died before he could take up the post. Through his connections and canny use of political office he is a living example of late-nineteenth-century Brazil's system of *coronelismo*, or 'colonelism', when power was concentrated in the hands of landowners who essentially ran everything.

When Brazil abolished slavery in 1888 there was no substantial land reform and after the Brazilian empire crumbled, in 1889, the all-powerful economic elite remained in firm control. The First Republic was officially organized by a rural oligarchy nicknamed 'coffee and milk' with the presidency rotating between the coffee barons of São Paulo and farmers from Minas Gerais. The military junta that took power in 1930 was run by Getúlio Vargas, a member of one of the old cattle families. The last president before the 1964 military coup, the reformist democrat João Goulart, was a landowner on a massive scale, but his toleration of left-wingers and his government's attempts to limit multi-nationals moved the military to seize control, suspending democratic elections until 1985 and Sarney's consequent rule.

Even after democracy took root and flowered, regional dominance by a single man or family was common. Sarney's daughter, Roseana, has been Maranhão's governor and sits in the Senate. His son was a minister in Brazil's previous government. Other relatives are scattered in positions of power across Maranhão's courts and the civil service. One of Sarney's trusted lieutenants, Edison Lobão, is Lula's Minister of Mines and Energy. When he won the job, Lobão's seat in the national Senate went to his son; his wife, meanwhile, sits in the lower house.

In February 2009, with Lula's support, Sarney was picked as chairman of the Senate. It is the third time in his career that he has held this powerful job, which confers a degree of control over the government's agenda and opportunities for patronage. Opposition politicians accuse Sarney of a range of dodgy deals, and they're clamouring for him to step down.

Federal police began investigating some of the claims but Sarney denies wrongdoing and says he doesn't plan to resign. His two chief defenders in the Senate are Renan Calheiros, a former Senate chairman making a comeback after taking a leave of absence to fight a corruption scandal, and Fernando Collor, Brazil's former president, who was impeached in 1992. Lula is backing this dubious duo.

Over the summer, thousands of Brazilians demonstrated against Sarney in co-ordinated protests in 13 cities across the country. In São Paulo, 1,000 demonstrators wore red noses and stopped traffic. The protesters are using comedy as a weapon, as all else seems to have failed. One arm of the campaign is called Rir Para Não Chorar (Laugh Not to Cry). 'The clown's nose is a legitimate symbol of society's defence and integrity,' according to Fernanda Suplicy, an organizer who claims that 50,000 red noses have been distributed on São Paulo's streets. Given charges are being dropped almost as fast as they are issued, it's one of the few means left.

At first glance, the new globalized, cost-cutting, acquisitive billionaires may seem very different from Sarney's decrepit land-based oligarchy centred on Maranhão – but it's purely stylistic, according to Alex Bellos, author of *Futebol: The Brazilian Way of Life*:

> Money and power, old or new, still buy influence. The main difference between the two is style, I'd say. It's very important to note that old money tends to have political power that is translated into business success often through business concessions. New money tends to involve

businessmen who could translate money into political power. It's the same but the opposite.

Batista, for instance, is in many ways the public face of Brazil's new rich. He's a former powerboat champion who broke various speedboat records between 1990 and 2006 and photographs of his ocean racing powerboats line the walls of his office on Flamengo beach – which also has a breathtaking view of Guanabara Bay. Clearly a speed freak, he keeps a Mercedes-Benz SLR McLaren racing car parked in his living room. He takes a daily vitamin cocktail intravenously to stave off ageing, holding meetings in his office with the fluids dripping into his left arm from an intravenous bag hanging on a pole with the green, yellow and blue Brazilian flag. His luxury yacht takes paying customers on sightseeing trips along Rio's coast and all his companies have an X in their name – he holds a superstition that it will multiply his wealth. There's OGX Petroleo e Gas Participacoes, EBX holdings, TVX Gold, MMX mining and TXX, the ports operator. All his oil bids ended in 63 cents – 63 being his lucky number.

'Batista is first and foremost a showman,' explains Alex Bellos. 'Brazilians love a showman – they're outgoing and like extroverts. You get nowhere in Brazil by being modest.' Indeed, most of Brazil's super-rich have a flamboyant touch. Polo player and playboy Ricardo Mansur, for instance, has dated models Gisele Bundchen, Isabeli Fontana and actress Luana Piovani and runs a complex series of interlocking businesses from his polo team to the night-club Café de la Musique.

Or take Dr Ivo Pitanguy, the country's leading plastic surgeon in a developing nation that boasts more cosmetic surgeons than any country outside the US. The good doctor has earned so much from his work at Rio's Clínica Ivo Pitanguy that he owns an estate in the city, a chalet in Gstaad, an apartment in Paris and a private island off the coast of Brazil where he keeps his personal menagerie of rare animals and exotic birds. Those valued clients invited to the island take a private jet or helicopter from Rio along Copacabana and Ipanema beaches to Angra dos Reis, the 'Bay of the Kings', where Pitanguy's mile-long Ilha dos Porcos Grande lies. They stay in bungalows designed by Brazilian architect Paulo Coelho and sunbathe by the pool as they wait for the scars to recede.

Batista came into this clique as an outsider – a college drop-out with nothing but the ambition to become Brazil's richest person. He was born in Brazil but spent most of his youth in Europe with his German mother and six siblings, ultimately studying metallurgy at Aachen University in Germany before buying his first gold mine in the Amazon basin aged just 24. The mine was so rich it was almost idiot-proof and it earned him $6 million in the first year. It wasn't quite the Aluminium Wars, but owning a gold mine in the Amazon had a touch of the Wild West. He claims to have had his bodyguard kill a man who drew a gun in a dispute over money.[7] With this cash and limited experience he expanded into Chile, Canada and Russia, where he says he was kicked out by the Mafia, building and losing his first fortune on the way.

It appears to have been a galling experience. His charismatic father, Eliezer, was former Mining and Energy Minister of Brazil and served twice as chief executive at Brazilian mining giant Vale. This – along with his four-year marriage to a *Playboy* cover girl who left him for a fireman – fuels Batista's apparently limitless ambition. In 2009 he achieved his 'Brazil's richest man' dream after selling his Brazilian mines to Anglo American. That still leaves him with 689 million tons (700 million tonnes) of iron ore reserves, a bauxite project, ports, power plants, a water company and his oil and gas. His new goal is to become the world's richest man in five years.

'For years I was referred to as the husband of Luma de Oliveira and son of Eliezer Batista,' he said in 2008. 'I decided that it had to change, for my kids. I'm totally self-made and I want to be a reference in terms of thinking big, doing big things and I want to have a reputation in this country.'[8]

His father wouldn't let him get close to Vale, even when it was privatized, so with Oedipal finesse he purchased a stake in the company in autumn 2009 – possibly large enough to secure control. It's going to make him even richer. Lula believes Vale should move into steel production. Batista agrees. And there's an awful lot of steel needed to build those Olympic stadia.

Of course, Batista's relationship with Lula's government is entirely unofficial – the loan of his jet being merely a favour to those making Rio's Olympic bid. Curiously, however, in autumn 2009 Batista struck oil. Literally. His OGX Petroleo e Gas Participacoes oil company discovered 1.3 billion gallons (4.8 billion litres) of crude offshore in plots he had bid for at the edge of the Petrobras vast concession. In June 2008, despite more than 27 companies cancelling share flotations on Brazil's stock market, Batista's OGX had gone ahead with what turned out to be the largest in Brazil's history, even though it had yet to start drilling its undersea plots. It might have hit rock but everyone knew Batista would find something. In theory, when he had bid $1.12 billion for 21 undersea tracts, he couldn't have known for sure. The size of the Petrobras find was still under wraps when he began laying plans to bid heavily. Executives at mining giant Vale and state-owned Petrobras say it's pure good fortune and credit Batista's geologists – drawn from their own former cadres. Either way, Batista and the state work well together.

At the same time, if Sarney has had Lula and the Brazilian state cover his back for months, Batista hasn't done badly either. He was briefly investigated for corruption in July 2008 when police raided his home and office as part of a probe into fraud and tax evasion, alleging he had smuggled gold and unfairly influenced the granting of rights to run the Amapá Railroad. Two months later, however, Federal police chief Romero Menezes was arrested for leaking information about the anti-Batista operation. The case has since gone quiet, although Batista's response was that the investigation was simply a 'gigantic mistake'.

Yet as one oilman comments:

> In Brazil, it is a given that people doing business at that level call in favours, know their rivals and partners and the politicians and bankers involved very well, and must participate in the game. I am sure Eike has skeletons in his cupboard. The question is, how well can he play the game? Because if you can play the game skilfully without standing on too many powerful toes, you can get away with murder.

And this can be taken literally when it comes to Brazil's super-rich. In January 2009 police issued a second murder indictment against Constantino de Oliveira, the billionaire co-founder of Brazil's second largest airline Gol Linhas Aereas, accusing him of ordering the killings of two men in a 2001 land dispute near Brasília. Oliveira, who denied the charges, was placed under house arrest then released in July. It seems unlikely he'll ever face trial: the oldest case outstanding at Rio's Courts of Justice dates back to 1911.

As a result, the private sector effectively runs its own state. Alongside the vast private security industry that gives everyone of wealth their own armoured cars and armed bodyguards, companies like mining company Vale have their own railway lines. Vale's enables it to get its iron ore from Carajas to market without relying on the country's patchy state railway network.

The company is also a shareholder in MRS Logistica's company railway system in the south, along with steelmakers CSN and Usiminas. Just as in nineteenth-century America where Standard Oil and Carnegie Steel used their railroads as a weapon against their competitors, these companies use the speed, cost and efficiency of their private transport systems to dominate the country. Everyone else has to use the roads – with trucks over 24 years old decorated in prayers for safety and bumping across a network that has only 12 per cent of its roads covered in tarmac.

In theory, the government is investing in infrastructure. The 2014 World Cup will be held in Brazil, but it already looks as if some of the promises made, such as the construction of a high-speed railway line to connect Rio and São Paulo, will fail to materialize. In Brazil they have a joke about this. A Brazilian politician goes to France to stay with his French equivalent. The Paris house is a vast mansion, decorated in the latest style and dripping with wealth. 'I didn't know French politicians earned so much money,' our senator says. 'You see that bridge?' asks the Frenchman. He pats his pocket. 'Fifty per cent of the money went in here . . .'. Two weeks later, the visit is returned and the Frenchman is astonished to find the Brazilian mansion easily out-classes his own in its opulence. 'I didn't realize Brazilian politicians earned so much money,' gasps the European. 'You see that bridge?' asks Mr Brazil. 'I can't see any bridge,' puzzles the Frenchman. The Brazilian pats his pocket. 'One hundred per cent of the money went in here.'

Brazil's government and its billionaires expand hand in hand. Brazil, like China, is tying up deals in Africa – and trading with countries the United Nations recoils from. Lula is a firm friend of Iran, for instance. And his tyrant giants are moving into place to join the global feeding frenzy. Vale, Embraer jets, Petrobras, steelmakers Gerdau and CSN, construction firms Odebrecht and

Camargo Corrêa – these are already multi-national megacorps and, according to Boston Consulting, there's at least 34 on the way. In 2009 the government loaned over $8 billion to Brazilian companies purely to help them expand internationally.

And so we have an oligarch class that admits to or is accused of murder, endemic corruption, cosy deals between the state and themselves, a rapidly expanding power of undue influence with huge oil reserves and an ever increasing presence in essential commodities from minerals to food. Sound familiar? It's the way of the future if the BRIC countries' predicted dominance continues without political change.

In the face of this onslaught, therefore, it's important that the West stick to its democratic values, to show that, when the chips are down, a democracy that serves the will of *all* its people can serve them better, particularly in a time of crisis. That's surely the strongest defence against the march of the violently aggressive super-rich who are buying our planet and its resources. It's a shame we've already failed so alarmingly to prove anything close.

CHAPTER SEVEN

IN WHICH FRIENDS DON'T LET FRIENDS DRIVE THEIR COMPANIES INTO THE GROUND

Goldman Sachs' new global headquarters is a custom-built 43-storey skyscraper diagonally opposite Ground Zero at 200 West Street, New York, built over the course of 2007 and 2008. Despite the glaring presence of the gleaming steel and glass tower, no one at the global banking giant has ever spoken on record about their new home. An interview with the architect in the *New York Times* revealed that the building has six high-tech trading floors, thirty floors of office space and three floors of meeting and amenity space on the lower floors. The heart of the building is a kind of living-room for Goldman Sachs staff on the 10th and 12th floors, where exercise, dining and meeting areas are linked by a lobby and a sweeping three-storey stairway. The exterior boasts a 5,000 square feet (465 square metres) retail arcade with walkways connecting to surrounding buildings, shopping areas and the Hudson River.

Goldman Sachs' reticence is a little curious – especially as the $2.4 billion tower was financed with $1.65 billion tax-exempt Liberty Bonds given to the company as a post-911 incentive to stay downtown in the hope that other large firms would follow. In exchange, Goldman is expected to give $4.5 million to Lower Manhattan residents for a library and community recreation centre; $1.65 billion versus $4.5 million still looks like a very good deal. You'd expect Goldman Sachs to be saying thank-you to the taxpayers – at least once. But then, Goldman Sachs doesn't like saying thank-you to taxpayers, even when said taxpayer saves them from certain destruction. Goldman Sachs likes to plough its own lonely furrow – lonely apart from all the high-powered members of the New York/Washington political elite who worked there, trained there and appear determined to funnel cash its way come what may.

Indeed, in the summer of 2009, Goldman Sachs was identified as the chief player in what Simon Johnson, professor at MIT Sloan School of Management and former chief economist at the IMF, described as the world's 'most advanced oligarchy'. Writing in *Atlantic Monthly* in May 2009, he outlined the key similarities between the US economy and the dubious cronyism of the emerging world's super-rich. Johnson believes that this oligarchy not only helped create the distinctive nature of the 2008–09 recession – the wild risks on flawed investments that brought down banks and shut off credit – but also ensured those who engineered the crash did exceptionally well out of the chaos that followed. Johnson argued:

> Emerging-market governments and their private-sector allies commonly form a tight-knit – and, most of the time, genteel – oligarchy, running the country rather like a profit-seeking company in which they are the controlling shareholders. When a country like Indonesia or South Korea or Russia grows, so do the ambitions of its captains

of industry. As masters of their mini-universe, these people make some investments that clearly benefit the broader economy, but they also start making bigger and riskier bets. They reckon – correctly, in most cases – that their political connections will allow them to push on to the government any substantial problems that arise.[1]

John Plender, columnist for the *Financial Times*, agrees. During a day spent discussing financial elites at the London School of Economics he explained:

> We're seeing the formation of rigid controlling elites that match, in some ways, the enarques of France [the name it gives to its super-elite] or the Iron Triangle of Japan – although in both those cases there is a sense of public service and responsibility amongst their elites. The financial elites in Washington and London more closely resemble the corrupt elites of Third World countries – with the main difference being that in the US the corruption is conduct[ed] in plain view, while in the UK it is still hidden and furtive.

It's a persuasive comparison. The sub-prime mortgage bubble was created when a series of banking rules were swept away by senior bankers who had stepped into government positions, helped pass laws deregulating Wall Street, then left for lucrative posts in the financial sector they had liberalized. Their replacements – former CEOs from the same banks – handed out taxpayers' money to save their old employers, guarantee them healthy annual bonuses and allow a few distinctly peculiar share deals. If it didn't give the world a new Abramovich or Berezovsky, it did make a small group of men an awful lot of money at the expense of the ordinary citizen.

Johnson's IMF years meant he saw another deep and disturbing similarity between this crash and equivalent slumps in oligarch economies, which he outlined thus:

> . . . elite business interests – financiers, in the case of the US – played a central role in creating the crisis, making ever-larger gambles, with the implicit backing of the government, until the inevitable collapse. More alarming, they are now using their influence to prevent precisely the sorts of reforms that are needed, and fast, to pull the economy out of its nosedive. The government seems helpless, or unwilling, to act against them.[2]

Rolling Stone journalist Matt Taibbi goes further – he specifically links Goldman Sachs above all others to the crash:

> As George Bush's last Treasury secretary, former Goldman CEO Henry 'Hank' Paulson was the architect of the bailout, a suspiciously self-serving plan to funnel trillions of Your Dollars to a handful of his old friends on Wall Street. Robert Rubin, Bill Clinton's former Treasury Secretary, spent 26 years at Goldman before becoming chairman of Citigroup – which in turn got a $300 billion taxpayer bailout from Paulson. There's John Thain, the asshole chief of Merrill Lynch who bought an $87,000 area rug for his office as his company was imploding; a former Goldman banker, Thain enjoyed a multibillion dollar hand-out from Paulson, who used billions in taxpayer funds to help Bank of America rescue Thain's sorry company. And Robert Steel, the former Goldmanite head of Wachovia, scored himself and his fellow executives $225 million in golden parachute payments, as his bank was self-destructing. There's Joshua Bolten, Bush's chief of staff during the bailout, and Mark

Patterson, the current Treasury chief of staff, who was
a Goldman lobbyist just a year ago, and Ed Liddy, the
former Goldman director whom Paulson put in charge
of bailed out insurance giant AIG, which forked over
$13 billion to Goldman after Liddy came on board. The
heads of the Canadian and Italian national banks are
Goldman alums, as is the head of the World Bank, the head
of the New York Stock Exchange, the last two heads of the
Federal Reserve Bank of New York – which, incidentally,
is now in charge of overseeing Goldman.[3]

By Taibbi's charge, government intervention doesn't look
helpless or reluctant – it looks downright enthusiastic when it
comes to helping out a very specific group. The story begins
when the credit crunch bit on Friday 12 September 2008, and
US Treasury Secretary and former Goldman Sachs CEO Henry
Paulson called a number of Wall Street CEOs to an emergency
meeting at the New York Federal Reserve Bank with the aim
of hammering out a response to the collapsing markets – most
specifically the investment bank Lehman Brothers, which was
unlikely to survive the weekend without help.

Journalist Joe Hagan provides a persuasive insider descrip-
tion of the whole weekend in *New York Magazine*:[4] a line
of black town cars and SUVs carried CEOs Jamie Dimon
of JPMorgan, John Thain from Merrill Lynch, Vikram Pandit of
Citigroup, Brady Dougan from Credit Suisse, John Mack from
Morgan Stanley and Lloyd Blankfein, Paulson's successor at
Goldman Sachs, along Maiden Lane in Lower Manhattan and
into the basement of the Federal Reserve Bank's 17-storey
Italian Renaissance-style fortress.

Things were looking grim. Bear Stearns was dead, Merrill
Lynch was in desperate need of a saviour and Lehman Brothers
was on the brink. Lehman's chief executive Dick Fuld had spent

the past few days bombarding Ken Lewis, his counterpart at Bank of America, with phone messages pleading with him to use his stronger institution to mount a rescue. Fuld even persuaded George Walker, a non-executive director of Lehman who was a cousin of President Bush, to put in a call to the Oval Office with a last-ditch appeal for a bailout, over the head of Treasury Secretary Henry Paulson. The President refused to answer the phone.

Now, in the Federal Reserve Bank, Paulson asked Wall Street to come up with a private funding solution. The government, he said at the outset, would not bail out the firm. The cream of Wall Street were divided into groups, fuelled with coffee and hectored to work something out. By Sunday afternoon, with Paulson still determined the government wouldn't step in, there was no deal on the table.

Lehman Brothers prepared to declare bankruptcy, ending its 158-year run on Wall Street. Bank of America, meanwhile, held out its arms to Merrill Lynch and its CEO John Thain, a former Goldman Sachs man. Christopher Flowers, the billionaire founder of the private-equity firm J.C. Flowers & Co., oversaw the signing of the deal, earning him roughly $20 million. As it happens, Flowers had previously worked with Paulson at Goldman Sachs for 20 years.

When the financial markets awoke to the news that Lehman Brothers was going under there was predictable panic. If the US government wasn't going to bail out failed banks, any one of them could go under. The Dow Jones industrial average slumped by more than 500 points, its worst fall since the aftermath of the terrorist attacks of 11 September 2001. Shares also plunged in Europe, Taipei, Mumbai and Manila. In Britain, the value of shares in Halifax Bank of Scotland (HBOS) halved in the space of an hour. Desperate to stave off a second banking failure, the UK government suspended competition rules to broker a £12.2 billion merger with Lloyds TSB. Over in New York the run continued and continued until it threatened the American insurance giant AIG.

AIG – originally founded in Shanghai in 1919 and only moving to New York when Mao Zedong marched on the Chinese city – had begun in personal insurance but switched to corporate deals in the 1960s. By 2008, it was insuring huge numbers of credit default swaps – essentially meaning it was insuring vast corporate loans and credit deals. If the loan, mortgage or debt failed – if the debtor failed to pay, for instance – it was AIG's job to recompense the creditor.

The company had underwritten deals to the tune of billions of dollars and these had now pretty much all failed – meaning AIG had to pay up. Its financial situation was so parlous that if it tried to cover its obligations, it would run out of money very, very quickly. Late in the evening of 16 September – 48 hours after Lehman's bankruptcy – AIG admitted it was about to go bust. When it came to the problems faced by insurance giant AIG, however, an entirely different philosophy emerged in the US government.

Goldman Sachs was AIG's biggest Wall Street client, owed $13 billion by the insurer. With the jumpy market prepared to mount blistering runs on any bank looking weak, the loss of that $13 billion could have closed Goldman Sachs. At the meeting convened at the Federal Reserve Bank to discuss AIG, Goldman Sachs was represented on both the banking and the government sides of the conference table. The Goldman's in-house entourage was led by the bank's top brass: CEO Blankfein, co-chief operating officer Jon Winkelried, investment banking head David Solomon, and its top merchant banking executive, Richard Friedman – all of whom had worked closely with Henry Paulson two years before.

On the government side, Treasury Secretary Timothy Geithner had never worked for Goldman, but he was an acolyte of former Goldman co-chairman and Clinton Treasury Secretary Robert Rubin. Former Goldman vice-president Dan Jester served as Paulson's representative from the Treasury. And though Paulson himself wasn't present, he was acutely aware of Goldman's position in regard to AIG, since the original AIG deals were created under his command.[5] Between them, these men hammered out a deal that would see the government step in with $85 billion of taxpayers' money and take a majority stake in AIG. Most banks got 13 cents of each dollar they were owed. Goldman Sachs got its full $13 billion.

Why did Paulson bail out the banks that did business with AIG and not Lehman Brothers? Chairman of the United States Federal Reserve Ben Bernanke later told James Stewart at the *New Yorker*:

> AIG was even larger than Lehman, with a substantial presence in derivatives and debt markets, as well as insurance markets. Given the extent of the exposures of major banks around the world to AIG and in light of the extreme fragility of the system, there was a significant risk that AIG's failure could have sparked a global banking panic. If that had happened it was not at all clear we could have stopped the bleeding, given the resources and authorities we had available at the time.[6]

Executives at Lehman aren't entirely convinced by this argument. As one former director of Lehman's puts it:

> ... the consensus is that we were deliberately fucked. Whatever happened in that room over the weekend of the 12th September has become the subject of such huge speculation. There's a lot of Lehman's staff convinced that Goldman guys were very happy to remove a very big

competitor. What's true is that they ratcheted back their line of defence during those discussions. At the beginning, Lehman's was within the defensive position. At the end it was outside it. Was it a conspiracy? Who knows what emotions influence a decision like that. If you're Goldman's through and through, what do you really feel about saving Lehman?

In the UK there's also some reserve about the moment America chose to act. Hector Sants, chief executive of the Financial Services Authority, believes the collapse of confidence in the banking system was a direct result of Paulson's decision not to help Lehman Brothers:

> I have sympathy for the US authorities given the complexity of the problems they faced that weekend but I do believe it was a mistake to let Lehman's fail. Without the future market shock created by Lehman Brothers' collapse, RBS may not have failed. Was Lehman the cause or was it the manifestation? It was our view that if Lehman had been supported you would not have seen such a dramatic reduction in liquidity.[7]

Mitchel Abolafia, who researches monetary policy and politics at the Rockefeller College of Public Affairs and Policy, is more charitable. 'When it went down Paulson called together his best friends,' he believes. 'He had come up through Goldman and his friends were at Goldman. Was he right? Yes, he could talk and think freely with his friends. Did it give them undue influence? Absolutely.'

Paulson's future actions did nothing dispel the conspiracy theories. According to the *New York Times*, Paulson spoke to Lloyd Blankfein 24 times in the six days following the AIG crisis. He named Edward C. Forst, a former head of Goldman's investment management division, to help draft the $700 billion Toxic Asset Relief Program (of which $10 billion went to Goldman Sachs), and then Neel Kashkari, a former Goldman vice-president, as the programme's manager. Edward Liddy, a former Goldman board member, was already serving as the new CEO of AIG.[8]

It was about the time when Stephen Friedman, serving as both a board member at Goldman Sachs and chairman of the Federal Reserve Bank of New York, bought 52,600 shares of Goldman stock while he was supposed to be responsible for the firm's oversight that journalists started to grumble in print.

In July 2009, Goldman Sachs announced senior staff bonuses of $11.4 billion – slightly less than its AIG bailout – which caused widespread fury but, as Professor Simon Johnson of MIT could have predicted, resulted in precisely nothing happening. How could the bank have done something so politically inept? 'It's a statement of arrogance,' one former executive believes. 'They're saying: we're smarter than anybody else.' And the Goldman's workforce does need the money – it's not for nothing that its staff is said to consist of 'the haves, and the have-yachts'.

The outrageous personal quirks of America's oligarchs certainly compete with the likes of Berezovsky, Mittal and Batista. SAC Capital Partners top dog Steven A. Cohen buys the rights to photographs of himself in advance of any public appearance. It's hard to find his image even online. The idiosyncrasies don't stop there. Picked up by a chauffeur-driven car every morning from his $15 million 14-acre (5.6-hectare) compound in the leafy New England town of Greenwich, he's driven to SAC headquarters in nearby Stamford where his office is flanked by a 14-foot (4.3-metre) tiger shark preserved in formaldehyde. Moore Global Investments head Louis Bacon, meanwhile, prefers to kill his own dead things at an $11 million island just off the coast of New York, with 435 acres (176 hectares) used exclusively for pheasant-hunting parties.

'Wall Street is a very seductive place, imbued with an air of power,' Johnson explains, continuing :

> Its executives truly believe that they control the levers that make the world go round. A civil servant from Washington invited into their conference rooms, even if just for a meeting, could be forgiven for falling under their sway. Throughout my time at the IMF, I was struck by the easy access of leading financiers to the highest US government officials, and the interweaving of the two career tracks. I vividly remember a meeting in early 2008 – attended by top policy makers from a handful of rich countries – at which the chair casually proclaimed, to the room's general approval, that the best preparation for becoming a central bank governor was to work first as an investment banker.
>
> A whole generation of policy makers has been mesmerized by Wall Street, always and utterly convinced that whatever the banks said was true. Alan Greenspan's pronouncements in favour of unregulated financial markets are well known. Yet Greenspan was hardly alone. Ben Bernanke, the man who succeeded him, said – 'The management of market risk and credit risk has become increasingly sophisticated. . . . Banking organizations of all sizes have made substantial strides over the past two decades in their ability to measure and manage risks.'
>
> Of course, this was mostly an illusion. Regulators, legislators, and academics almost all assumed that the managers of these banks knew what they were doing. In retrospect, they didn't. AIG's Financial Products division, for instance, made $2.5 billion in pre-tax profits in 2005,

largely by selling underpriced insurance on complex, poorly understood securities. Often described as 'picking up nickels in front of a steamroller', this strategy is profitable in ordinary years, and catastrophic in bad ones. As of Fall 2008, AIG had outstanding insurance on more than $400 billion in securities. To date, the US government, in an effort to rescue the company, has committed about $180 billion in investments and loans to cover losses that AIG's sophisticated risk modelling had said were virtually impossible.[9]

Johnson's 'complex, poorly understood securities', variously described as, mortgage backed securities, collaterized debt obligations, derivatives – there are many, many names for these products, but they produced the same basic problem – was the strategy banks came up with to side-step new rules limiting the amount of money they could lend.

Under the terms of 2004's Basle II Accord, all lenders must have assets worth 8 per cent of their total loans. Thus they have to have, say, £8 billion in assets to lend £100 billion in mortgages, business loans and the like. At global investment bank level, lending money can include financing for vast projects like a nuclear power station in South Africa – a risky proposition that could cost up to £15 billion but would make a handsome profit for the lender. Some loans, however, tie up a chunk of a bank's assets in tediously long-term, low-risk and low-reward arrangements – like a mortgage.

'The thing about a mortgage is, it pays out interest over 25 years,' explains Bob Kelsey, chairman of Moorgate Group. 'That's a good business for a long-term investor like, say, a pension fund. They know they will get a steady flow of cash. For a bank, particularly an investment bank, it's really bad business. It's a small income over a long period of time.'

As a result, if you've taken out a mortgage in the last eight years, the chances are the bank has created a company – let's call it Penge Investments – stuffed your mortgage and a bunch of other loans into this company, then sold it as if it were a normal company. Selling the debts on means they are no longer owned by the bank so it can lend again against the assets it used to back your original mortgage. And again. And again.

For a while, pension funds and long-term investors were the main buyers for these bundles of debt. In 2001, however, an analyst at Barclays Capital called David X Li came up with a fiendishly complicated equation for pricing special-purpose vehicles like Penge Investments on the open market. Bob Kelsey explains:

> From 2001, investment banks and hedge funds were buying these vehicles as a trading asset, something that would rise in value on the market and they could sell on. So they were inventing the value of these things themselves and, in doing so, they were ignoring something incredibly fundamental. At the beginning of the century, the debt machines being sold to pension funds included some sort of security against defaults – if you estimate that on average 5 per cent of mortgages default, you add six more mortgages for every 100 in the bundle. But the rate of defaulting is hard to judge as an average by looking back over the last five years. What you find is that there are years of zero defaults, then there's an economic slump and you suddenly get a huge spike in the number of defaults. Banks looked back over five years, saw mortgage defaults were zero so stopped adding in any serious margins. The US government was encouraging a housing boom and pushing banks to lend to riskier customers. The banks started bundling up the risk and spreading it through the

financial system. Suddenly, in one year they had so many
defaults their margin of protection wasn't anywhere near
wide enough. As a result, as far as the market is concerned,
those vehicles are suddenly worth zero. So whatever the
bank paid for them and however they have them down on
their balance sheet – I've seen vehicles with $1 billion or
$2 billion worth of assets bundled up – when the sub-prime
mortgages started defaulting you take them to the market
and they're worth zero.

At the risk of recapping the obvious, for most of the twentieth
century home-buyers had to be able to produce a down payment of at least 10 per cent of the value of their purchase, show
a steady income and good credit rating, and possess a real first
and last name. At the end of the 1990s, a market had opened
that threw those 'dumb' ideas out of the window and eventually
created the downright hilarious NINJA mortgages – a thrilling
acronym for No Income, No Job or Assets. How could anyone
think this was a good idea?

In fact, some people could see this was a bad idea as far back
as 1998 – specifically Brooksley Born, then head of the US
Commodity Futures Trading Commission, who started asking
how derivatives could be regulated. She'd raised the idea that
banks be required to maintain greater reserves if they were to
deal in derivatives. She was also worried by the discreet way
these opaque deals were done and had pushed for far greater
transparency.

Federal Reserve Bank boss Alan Greenspan (ex-JPMorgan)
and Treasury Secretary Robert Rubin (ex-Goldman) had fun-
damentally disagreed. They'd called Born in for a meeting
and tried to dissuade her from further comments on the subject. She'd continued to push for more regulation. Rubin had
publicly denounced her suggestions and recommended that

Congress strip her Commission of its regulatory authority. In 2000, on its last day in session and with effectively zero debate, Congress had passed the now-notorious Commodity Futures Modernization Act, inserted into an 11,000-page spending bill. The Act accepted specific recommendations from Greenspan, Rubin and the new Commodities Futures Trading Commission chairman William Ranier that derivatives be exempt from regulation. Banks could trade them with impunity.

In other words, when one regulator Born tried to gain control of a wild bubble market that she saw could lead to speculation and a crash, ex-bankers – who seemed keen to ensure their one-time colleagues could keep profiting from the bubble's resistible rise – stymied her.

For John Plender of the *Financial Times* (*FT*) it wasn't just old firm ties:

> Between 1998 and 2008 Wall Street made $1.27 billion in political donations and spent another $3.4 billion on lobbyists paying, for example, around 3,000 officially registered Federal lobbyists to work for the industry in 2007 – roughly five lobbyists for every member of Congress. This was all to persuade government not to regulate the financial markets. The moving staircase – Wall Street moving up into the administration – helped, but it took the lobbying and donations to make sure Born's plan was nipped in the bud.

Alan Greenspan's memoir *The Age of Turbulence* outlines his beliefs:

> It seems superfluous to constrain trading in some of the newer derivatives and other innovative financial contracts of the past decade. The worst have failed; investors no longer fund them and are not likely to in the future.

Essentially the Federal Reserve Bank had decided that it wholeheartedly supported private banks, accepted the wisdom of the market and handed Wall Street a laissez-passer. The Rockefeller's Mitchel Abolafia – who has trawled through transcripts of those meetings for his books on policy-making at the Federal Reserve Bank – explains:

The Fed simply doesn't consider Congress when it has its six-weekly meetings. It only discusses the views of the markets. It certainly doesn't worry about democratic interests or Congressmen – the attitude is 'What are they going to do to us? Shut us down?' It is not threatened and doesn't feel that it is threatened. There is a right way to talk and think. You notice this with Clinton's appointee Ned Gramlich, who left after 18 months because he'd speak and the next person would simply move on to another subject. The same thing happened with Nancy Teeters, the first woman to serve as governor. She said that once she'd spoken at a meeting, no one commented and the meeting moved on. She was ignored. This is not a range of American opinion.

Meanwhile, other former Goldman employees were helping their old buddies along. AIG had approached the New York State Insurance Department in 2000 and asked whether default swaps would be regulated like insurance. At the time Neil Levin, a former Goldman Sachs vice-president, ran the department. He'd decided against regulation, thus allowing AIG to fill its boots.

With AIG underwriting as many housing-based securities and offering as much credit default protection as it wanted, Goldman had been lending with glee. By the peak of the housing boom in 2006, the bank had been underwriting

$76.5 billion worth of mortgage-backed securities – a third of which were sub-prime – much of it to institutional investors like pensions and insurance companies. And in these massive issues of real estate there were acres of worthless properties paid for by people with no money and no foreseeable source of money.

Just after the crash an e-mail circulated City inboxes, with Heidi's Bar in the subject field, comparing the situation to one everyone could understand – booze. Heidi runs a bar in Berlin, the e-mail explained, and, to increase sales, allows her unemployed alcoholic clients to keep a tab. Sales increase massively as a result and her bank manager suggests she borrow money against the value of these tabs to expand the bar. She does. More people come. More tabs are arranged. The bank decides to sell stakes in her rapidly increasing bar bills to other banks. Sales are still increasing, the value of the tabs is still rising so the price of these stakes keeps rising until one day one of the bankers decides to ask one of the alcoholics to settle his tab. Of course they cannot pay. In the ensuing panic, Heidi and her suppliers go bankrupt and the government, following dramatic round the clock consultations by leaders of the governing political parties, steps in to save her bank. The funds required for this purpose, the e-mail concludes dryly, are obtained by a tax levied on non-drinkers.

Round the clock consultations by leaders from the governing political parties also saved Goldman Sachs. Of course, Lehman can't shirk blame for its own predicament. With $18 billion of core equity on its balance sheet, the bank had taken positions on an astonishing $780 billion in mortgages, stocks, bonds, oil, gold, derivatives and other investments. In 2007 it was leveraged 30 to 1 – meaning it had loaned $30 for every tangible dollar asset it possessed. By 2008 it had leveraged its books by an astonishing factor of 44 and it had opted to take a particularly huge punt on America's teetering home loans market. Northern Rock's predicament was caused by its reliance on derivatives to expand its lending. Indeed, every bank that required a bailout or went bankrupt had gambled on this market and lost.

Which is why MIT's Simon Johnson and Karel Williams of Manchester University's Centre for Research on Socio-Cultural Change are keen to remind everyone that Goldman Sachs and Co. were not only beneficiaries of government largesse, but that they used their political connections to create the financial crisis in the first place – demolishing the safeguards and regulations that could have prevented it through donations, lobbying and friends on the inside. They were hampered by rules that prevented them making more and more money in established markets so did all they could to avoid examination of a series of secretive and unregulated trades that triggered the 2008 recession. That line of town cars and SUVs turning into the basement garage of the Federal Reserve Bank held the small group of men who between them had devised the system that caused the crash, worked in the administrations that prevented regulation and then drew government money to cover their losses. That line of town cars could have been a line of Zils in Moscow, taking the oligarchs to help Yeltsin decide on his successor.

Come the new boss – he's the same as the old boss. Financial writer Michael Lewis points out that the Obama administration, led by Timothy Geithner and the White House's National Economic Council director Larry Summers, continues to believe in Goldman Sachs.[10] Goldman also has a key ally in Obama's chief of staff, Rahm Emanuel, a former investment banker and one-time adviser to Goldman Sachs who frequently solicited campaign funds from the firm while working with the Clintons. (Fans of the LA satire *Entourage* will recognize Rahm's brother Ari in the fictional character Ari Gold.) And in mid-July 2009, the same week Goldman Sachs announced massive second quarter profits, the administration quietly hired Robert Hormats, another Goldman executive, as Under Secretary for Economic, Energy and Agricultural Affairs in Hillary Clinton's Department of State.

That month, with unemployment rising and the British Chambers of Commerce reporting that cash flow was at its lowest since records began, Goldman Sachs posted the best results earned in its 140-year history. Revenue was up 65 per cent to $13.8 billion – roughly $38 million per day – with profits of $3.44 billion. Goldman paid out almost half of its earnings in staff bonuses – a compensation fund of $6.65 billion, or $226,000 for each employee.

Max Keiser, film-maker, broadcaster and former options trader, reacted to the results by calling Goldman Sachs 'scum'. He fumed:

> They basically have co-opted the US government, they've co-opted the Treasury department, the Federal Reserve, the Obama administration – Barack Obama dances to Goldman Sachs' tune – and what they've done is abominable. Hank Paulson held Congress hostage, took them into a back room and said, give us $700 billion or we're going to crash this market. America has for some reason allowed this *coup d'état* to take place where Goldman Sachs and their friends now manipulate and control the US government.

The Rockefeller College's Mitchel Abolafia remarks:

> I am surprised that Congress isn't holding hearings where the Fed is attacked. I think change will be minor and will leave the oligarchy in place. They are very efficient at damping down the discussion and leaving the structures in

place. We'd need a revolutionary change and I don't see that. Keynesianism was a revolution, Reaganism was a revolution, but I don't think that will happen now.

Goldman Sachs, however, still had one last piece of sleight of hand to reveal. It had sold sub-prime mortgage investments to its clients for years, but over the summer of 2009 it came out that in 2006 Goldman had begun trading against sub-prime on its own balance sheet without telling anyone, a hedge that ultimately let it profit when the market collapsed. For some, this was prescient; for others, a glaring conflict of interest and inherently dishonest, since the firm let its clients take the fall. For others again, it was just business: if Goldman knew everyone was buying toxic assets, why not keep on selling them? As John Whitehead, the godfather of Goldman Sachs' modern culture, wrote in a set of guidelines for executives: 'Important people like to deal with other important people. Are you one?'[11]

Professor Simon Johnson's fears over a financial oligarchy – and the depths of Goldman's links with the heart of the US government – may seem thousands of miles away to the British – but we have no reason to feel smug. In November 2009, the *Daily Mirror* listed the super-rich backers of the Conservative Party: billionaire broker Michael Spencer, hedge fund magnates Stanley Fink and Michael Hintze, Next boss Simon Wolfson and textile heir Andrew Feldman donated over £3 million between them, while millionaire non-dom party chairman Lord Ashcroft handed over £1.8 million – and pointed out that Tory plans to cut inheritance tax would be especially beneficial to '18 millionaire members of the shadow cabinet'.[12]

Any argument that the British political class is above undue financial influence is clearly fatuous in the light of various cash-for-honours, cash-for-questions and expenses-fiddling scandals among MPs. No doubt these donors will get the breaks they need. After all, if even the Labour Party, its former leader Tony Blair and its tax and spend chancellor Gordon Brown hocked themselves to the UK's financial oligarchs and freely distributed the kind of favours usually reserved for banana republics or Goldman Sachs employees, what hope is there for David Cameron?

CHAPTER EIGHT

IN WHICH THE BRITISH OLIGARCHS RELUCTANTLY STEP FORWARD

In Moscow, of course, they only have Russian oligarchs to deal with. In Mumbai, it's Indian money that concerns the authorities. Brazil's corruption battles are a local affair, while China won't let anyone else in on their financial games. Even campaigning US journalists only fear the consequences of American financiers manipulating the American economy. The UK, however, is special – it has all of the above plus an oligarchy of its very own.

There's a trail of blood that comes with the Russians – Litvinenko and his polonium, obviously, as well as some strange, unexplained deaths: the mysterious helicopter crash of Stephen Curtis, the British lawyer who was acting for the Russian oil company Yukos; an elderly British man shot dead outside his home, perhaps because he had been mistaken for a magistrate who continued to refuse extradition requests from Putin for Badri Patarkatsishvili, the British-based Georgian oligarch later found dead at his home in Leatherhead after an apparent heart attack – although police treated the death as suspicious.

And then there are the favours the British cut these foreign oligarchs: 2001's letter from Blair to the Romanian Prime Minister in support of Lakshmi Mittal, or the Hinduja passports scandal which caused the then Northern Ireland Secretary Peter Mandelson to resign after it was revealed the brothers were given British passports shortly after donating money to the Millennium Dome.

Or take Mandelson's controversial appearance on Russian metals magnate Oleg Deripaska's yacht in summer 2008. Mandelson rejected suggestions of a conflict of interest despite his role as European commissioner in charge of aluminium and Deripaksa's extensive aluminium interests: 'He [Deripaska] has never asked for any favours, I have never given him any favours and that is what the European Commission in their examination of the issue has very firmly put on record', Mandelson insisted to *Sky News* in October 2008.

Oleg was equally indignant: 'I wasn't considering in those days whether they were British politicians,' he told *Newsnight* on 14 July 2009. 'It was my summer holiday. We had a good dinner, there were many people and I'm surprised they picked on these poor guys and screwed them in the press.' When asked if he ever benefited from his relationship with Mandelson he became angry. 'Benefited from friendship? Whatever I did in my life, I did myself.'

Of course it's not just the Labour Party. In a letter to *The Times*, on 21 October 2008, shortly after the scandal broke, Nathaniel Rothschild, a hedge fund manager and member of the Rothschild banking dynasty who was also present on the yacht, expressed concern that the paper had focused on Mandelson and Deripaska while sparing an opposition MP – his college friend and shadow Chancellor of the Exchequer George Osborne:

Not once in the acres of coverage did you mention that George Osborne ... found the opportunity of meeting

with Mr [Oleg] Deripaska so good that he invited the
Conservatives' fundraiser Andrew Feldman, who was
staying nearby, to accompany him on to Mr Deripaska's
boat to solicit a donation. Since Mr Deripaska is not
a British citizen, it was suggested by Mr Feldman, in
a subsequent conversation at which Mr Deripaska was not
present, that the donation was 'channelled' through one of
Mr Deripaska's British companies. Mr Deripaska declined
to make any donation.

The Conservative Party denied Rothschild's claim, insisting that
when the possibility of a donation was raised by Rothschild –
whose mother Lady Serena Rothschild gave £190,000 to help
fund the shadow chancellor's office in 2007 – Feldman had said
there were strict rules on donations to political parties in the UK.

The bald truth is, however, that British politics of every hue
feeds on the donations of the non-domicile super-rich. Of the
£188 million raised by political parties between 2001 and 2008,
some £17.5 million came from those who declared themselves
to be non-domicile. Labour took a healthy £8.9 million from
non-doms while the Tories did slightly worse with £5.6 million. Labour receives cash from Gordon Brown's confidant
and the unelected Financial Services Secretary, popularly
known as Minister for the City, Lord Paul Myners, packaged
food tycoon Sir Gulam Noon, Lakshmi Mittal and Sir Ronald
Cohen, the godfather of British private equity. Among the Tory
non-dom donors is disgraced newspaper baron Conrad Black,
Hans Rausing, the Tetra Pak tycoon, and Lord Ashcroft. The
Liberal Democrats have Indian businessmen Bhanu and Dhruv
Choudhrie stumping up cash. It's no surprise that when back-
benchers forced through a law limiting non-dom party donations to £7,500 per year, the government delayed enacting it
until after the 2010 general election.

With all the benefits they receive, you'd expect non-doms to be contributing something significant to the economy. But then witness the embarrassing chaos over non-domicile tax rates. In 2008 – the year London for the first time became the EU's richest region, surpassing Luxembourg, Frankfurt and Paris – the TUC published research which showed that wealthy individuals and big business were costing the Treasury £25 billion through sophisticated tax avoidance measures. As a result, the government finally changed the law in an astonishing fudge that would cripple middle managers on international placements but have no effect whatsoever on the super-rich.

From 2008 non-domiciled UK residents still pay tax only on overseas income – but if they have been resident in the UK for at least 7 out of the past 10 years, they must pay £30,000 each year to ensure they retain their non-dom status. If they don't pay the £30,000, all of their income becomes eligible for tax. Imagine the hole that £30,000 would make in Mittal's $20 billion, Abramovich's $9 billion or Sir Philip Green's $5 billion . . .

Of course, this being Britain, money can't buy direct influence. Or can it? In early 2009 I met a senior civil servant attached to Number 10 Downing Street who had noticed the overwhelming number of high net worth individuals:

> . . . in the constant orbit of the government. You do see a number of Russian exiles meeting with cabinet ministers, although that has slightly decreased recently as ministers do their due diligence. None the less, key individuals with key contacts can pretty much walk into the rooms they want. Indian industrialists are particularly in attendance, they probably have the edge over Russians. You noticed that really pick up under the Blair administration and it has continued under Brown. What you also notice is the way ministers' wives are part of the chain of access. Charities

are a very obvious forum, so the wives of the wealthy invite the wives of ministers – or vice versa – to charitable events and then the husbands' conversations are all about business and politics. Sarah Brown's postbag produces a constant stream of invitations to the weddings of American fund managers or super-rich kids.

And it's not just an overseas phenomenon. There is a new and pervasive group of power players entering Whitehall from the UK as well, as the civil servant explains:

The new generation of fund managers, private equity kids and private corporation owners find it far easier to get ministerial access than MPs or junior ministers. Perhaps it's more visible – perhaps the old school tie or private club relationships of Conservatives meant it happened away from the corridors of power. It will be interesting to see what happens under a change of administration. I'm not privy to the party level, but it's clear the money is backing both horses – either leader is a loss leader, if you like. That's how the parties – which were both overloaded with hideous debt in the early nineties – are now debt-free. It certainly didn't come from the membership.

Of course, why wouldn't government ministers need to keep in touch with leading industrialists? Even so, the civil servant – who has served under various administrations for many years – feels something has changed significantly.

The characters you see now are the names and faces that only have resonance on the financial pages or in the *FT*. They're the people who buy things rather than build them from scratch. There's the feeling that you've seen a slightly

insidious takeover of the heights of the economy by people
we know very little about, and the links between them and
government are cosier than ever before.

At this point, of course, it is vital to pull up and avoid entering
the world of the conspiracy theory. It would be beyond idiotic
to imagine a secret cabal of international bankers – really alien
lizards in disguise – who are plotting to take over the world and
condemn us all to salt mines for eternity. The fact that oligarchs
and ministers know each other, visit each other and spend time
with each other is not the symptom of some vast plot. Every
manoeuvre outlined above should be seen as a series of rational
choices by individuals who have largely arrived at their position
through a combination of historical accident, good luck and
ferocious wit and tenacity. If you were to own a multi-national
company, you would be a fool not to cultivate the regulators
and the law-makers who decide your corporate future. Senior
employees of Goldman Sachs would not have gained their positions had they been the kind of people who would roll over at
a market crash rather than fight for their company's survival all
the way up to the Treasury Secretary and the President of the
United States. However, events do not have to be a conspiracy
for them to act against the best interests of the majority of the
population.

The discussions to save Goldman Sachs at the New York
Federal Reserve Bank were fuelled by coffee and crumb cake
as politicians and bankers swapped money around. In London,
it was a £245 takeaway from Gandhi's in Kennington, south
London – rice, karahi lamb, tandoori chicken, vegetable curry
and aloo gobi – that fed the chancellor Alistair Darling and lawyers and executives from Britain's eight leading banks during
their late-night discussion on 7 October when they haggled out
the terms of the government bailout.

It was a motley crew: Sir Fred Goodwin – 'Fred the Shred' – the millionaire boss of the Royal Bank of Scotland; Barclays boss John Varley; Eric Daniels, the American in charge of Lloyds TSB; and HBOS chief Andy Hornby, a former management consultant. HSBC sent a junior executive, just to prove they didn't need the money.

Lord Paul Myners, the white-haired, short-tempered Minister for the City, oversaw the discussions. The adopted son of a Truro butcher and hairdresser – he spent the first three years of his life in an orphanage in Bath – Myners had several incarnations on his way to the cabinet: as a trainee *Telegraph* journalist, as a fund manager in the City, as chair of Tate Trustees and as the man who saved Marks & Spencer from Philip Green. In the midst of global financial carnage, Gordon Brown rushed through a peerage so Myners could join the cabinet – although one of his companies, the hedge fund company GLG, quite legally made big profits by selling short tens of millions of shares in Bradford & Bingley as it teetered on the brink, and – as chairman of Aspen Insurance Holdings, a Bermuda-based insurance company – he spent five years avoiding more than £100 million a year in tax.

Indeed, if British politics had been lacking the US presence of a Wall Street chief in policy-making positions, Brown has more than compensated – appointing in June 2007 private equity chief Damon Buffini, Tesco chief executive Sir Terry Leahy and Lord Sir Alan Sugar, among others, to be a 'Business Council for Britain'. To further link the business sector to government policy, he recruited 'business ambassadors', including Marcus Agius, the chairman of Barclays, Sir Victor Blank, chairman of Lloyds TSB, Sir John Bond, chairman of Vodafone and Lord Browne of Madingley, the former BP chief executive and managing director of Riverstone, a private equity group.

The best face we can put on these events is that the government needs expert advice from respected City names because UK plc needs the City to survive. This, however, is not entirely true. In fact, the tax revenues from the finance sector in recent years were offset by the immediate cost of the massive bank bailouts. According to figures from the University of Manchester in the five years up to 2006/7, the finance sector paid and collected £203 billion in taxes, but the upfront costs of the UK bailout were £289 billion, rising potentially to £1,183 billion.[1] Over the last ten years or so, the City has bankrolled those parts of Britain's political parties that our foreign oligarchs can't reach, but whatever they paid – however many millions – it was like emptying a cup into the ocean of cash that the government hurled back at them as the financial crisis hit.

In terms of job creation, the finance sector directly employs no more than 1 million workers – mainly on the high street — and those numbers don't increase during boom years. If we add jobs in consultancy, accounting and law that are sustained by finance, the number of those directly and indirectly employed still accounts for no more than 6.5 per cent of the UK workforce, according to the Manchester University figures.

So if there's little benefit to the economy from the intimacy of this relationship, then who does stand to gain? *FT* journalist John Plender explains:

> Part of the power the City has over British politicians is fear. There's the tax the City pays and the belief that if the government over-regulates, the banks will leave, taking all their jobs with them. The numbers don't actually back that up. The City only accounts for 8 per cent of the UK's GDP, provides maybe a million jobs, and the tax receipts received over the last five years have all been wiped out by the bailouts. We've seen the intellectual subordination

> of state actors to business interests. What should define
> the relationship between the regulator or government and
> the market is adversarial legalism – the SEC [Securities
> and Exchange Commission], for instance, used to enforce
> regulations vigorously but that's been eroded by an ideo-
> logical faith in deregulation and the power of the market.

And it gets worse. There's a very strong and very specific relationship between the most rapacious arm of the City and the
Prime Minister himself. Lord Myners himself has never donated
directly to the Labour Party, but in 2007 he gave £12,700 to
Gordon Brown's leadership campaign. To be fair, he wasn't
alone. According to the Electoral Commission, Brown raised
£113,000 from Lord Paul, a Labour peer and owner of Caparo
Industries; Lord Bhattacharyya, another Labour peer, who
finances the £100 million Warwick University manufacturing
group; Lord Gavron, former chairman of the Guardian Media
Group; veteran City financier Sir Sigmund Sternberg; and
Community, the trade union that represents steelworkers, knit-
wear workers and cobblers. Shortly after Brown took charge,
private equity chiefs Sir Ronald Cohen and Nigel Doughty,
former Goldman Sachs partner Jon Aisbitt and internet betting
tycoon Peter Coates piled in – donating hundreds of thousands
of pounds to party coffers.

Why would the private equity industry bankroll a leadership
bid from a Labour Chancellor of the Exchequer? Perhaps out of
gratitude. The rise of the private equity industry is probably the
closest equivalent the UK has to the Goldman Sachs oligarchy.
One company in three sold in the UK is bought by private
equity; outside the public sector, one British employee in five
works for a company owned by private equity funds. In the past
25 years, the industry has grown from almost nothing to some
200 companies doing deals worth more than £20 billion a year.[2]

Private equity companies are vultures to venture capital's farmers. They borrow money to buy stock-market-listed companies in largely hostile bids. They dump their resulting debt on to the company's balance sheet. They then break the company up, sell off its crown jewels, sack its employees and restructure wherever possible until – after a few years – they've dispersed its constituent parts in tiny little pieces, at a fraction of its former glory but at a massive increase in its price.

The huge profits earned by these asset-strippers are almost entirely fuelled by legislation created by Gordon Brown. In 1998, when he was still chancellor, Brown introduced taper relief – a reduction in the tax entrepreneurs had to pay on business assets or shares they owned. The idea was to encourage entrepreneurs to invest. Taper relief reduced the capital gains tax on investments held for ten years to just 10 per cent. And the biggest beneficiaries were the people who run private equity firms who, thanks to Gordon Brown, benefited from the tax even though they quite clearly do the opposite of investing.

Karl-Heinz Spiegel at the London office of the trade union alliance the Anglo-German Foundation points to research by German unions showing private equity funds not only stop investment in new capital equipment, they also cut research and development:

> The purchase of Germany's FTE Automotive by private equity firm Hg Capital . . . [and its subsequent sale to] PAI Partners shows many of the negative outcomes . . . First, the company's balance sheet was loaded with the debt used to finance the buy-out. Management used operating cash flow to repay the debt, leading to an absolute decline in investment for research and development and new capital equipment. What they wanted to do was have the machine run for longer hours rather than upgrade the machines to

provide more output. They had so much debt already that it actually hinders investment. As a result, the workforce faced longer working hours, the abolition of Christmas and holiday pay, and 250 production jobs were moved to Eastern Europe.

'They justify shedding the labour force as something that corporations already do in order to meet shareholder value,' says Dr Johnna Montgomerie at the University of Manchester's Centre for Research on Socio-Cultural Change. 'It's not that it's unique to them in that sense.' She continues:

> They just pick up a thread. In order to make a company more valuable we need to shed workers. It's the logic of permanent restructuring, because even when a corporation is making a huge profit they need to shed 10 per cent of the workforce. They begin restructuring the rest of the business – for instance with Sainsbury's they liked the idea of 'leasing back', which means taking all the company's property assets, selling them and then renting them back again. That's financial engineering on a massive, secretive and often pointless scale.

When selling a financially engineered business on, private equity partners typically receive 20 per cent of the profit. It's a performance fee – the more money you get for flogging a company's wares, the larger your 20 per cent. Under the taper relief system, this money is taxed as a capital gain and is thus eligible for taper relief. The asset-stripping had somehow entered the taxation system as a form of investment.

In 2002, Brown modified the rules to allow people to become eligible for taper relief after only two years. Inevitably there were chancers who took advantage of the reduced time limit and the Treasury uncovered a flood of dodgy schemes designed to cash in. As a result, it tightened the rules of eligibility for everyone – except, that is, the sabre-toothed private equity firms, who somehow negotiated a special exemption in 2003, returning to their 10 per cent or less tax rate.

Bloomberg analyst Matthew Lynn argues:

> The way the private equity industry in particular has bank-rolled both parties is just extraordinary. And you don't know why they don't pay any tax or why Gordon Brown is so keen to preserve that tax break or how the Prime Minister has such good mates at private equity funds. Gordon Brown's leadership campaign was funded by private equity and the Tory Party has huge donors from hedge funds and private equity. The tax breaks they get are huge – I don't think anyone in the City thinks it's a good idea. They think it's a bit of wheeze but they don't really think it makes the country very efficient. Meanwhile these funds own the bulk of the economy. You cannot get through your day without giving money to several private equity funds but you have no idea who these people are or how they got their money.

However the deal was secured – lobbying, personal relationships or a sense of obligation from handsomely-funded politicians – the private equity industry grew exponentially as a result of these tax breaks. CVC Capital's £11.4 billion bid for J. Sainsbury and the £11 billion bidding war between Kohlberg Kravis Roberts and Terra Firma for Alliance Boots set the stage. From then on, no household name was beyond private equity's reach. A list of the biggest 170 deals done by private equity firms over the past three years alone includes the takeover of David Lloyd gyms, Travelodge Hotels, the Tussauds Group,

Birds Eye frozen foods, Pret A Manger, Fat Face clothing, Foxtons estate agents, Phones4U, Jimmy Choo, Leeds Bradford International Airport, Costcutter, La Senza and Vue Cinemas.

Take 'Business Council for Britain' member Damon Buffini. His company Permira has worked its way through the AA, New Look, Homebase and Birds Eye. Buffini's tale is instructive. Born in 1962 in a council flat in Leicester to his gas board worker mum Maureen and black American serviceman father Jonathan – who left fairly swiftly afterwards – he rose on the back of his mother's devotion. Maureen took a job in Leicester's Grand Hotel and moved her family into a two-up, two-down near the Victoria Park campus of Leicester University. Damon won a place at Gateway, a Leicester boys' grammar school specializing in engineering and industrial drawing, where he shone in the classroom as well as on the sports field. At parents' evenings, if Maureen was told Damon was doing well, she would ask how he could do better.

He studied law at Cambridge, took an MBA at Harvard and in 1988 started working for Schroder Ventures, cutting his teeth on increasingly large buy-outs. When, in 2001, the investment banking parent of Schroder sold its private equity operation, Buffini lead a management buy-out to form Permira. In the following five years it backed 14 European takeovers, each worth more than £500 million, and arranged 300 deals worth in the region of £40 billion, raising Buffini's personal fortune to around £200 million.

True to form, when Permira swoops asset-stripping follows. Buffini's purchase of Little Chef resulted in mass closure of restaurants. When he bought Birds Eye, there were assurances that jobs and terms and conditions would remain unchanged for three years. Less than a year later, he closed the Birds Eye food factory in Hull – losing 600 jobs – and moved production to Bremerhaven in Germany. After he took over the AA in 2004 he sacked 3,400 workers, including disabled staff, and raised membership charges by 30 per cent – doubling profits to £200 million and paying his fund a £500 million special dividend but burdening the AA with debts of £1.9 billion.

The GMB, Britain's third biggest union, fought back over the AA job losses by seeking to trash Buffini's personal reputation. 'Before we found out about Buffini, he was a hidden man,' explains the GMB's Paul Maloney. 'He'd just made thousands of people redundant but nobody knew about him. He was the spirit behind the evil, as it were. So we decided to make him the focus of our campaign.'

The resulting attacks were quite shocking and deeply personal. Buffini is a devout Christian, so the union picketed the Holy Trinity church in Clapham where he worships with his wife Deborah and their three young children. Protesters had a camel and signs referencing Matthew 19:24: 'It is easier for a camel to go through the eye of a needle than for a rich man to enter heaven.' Newspaper adverts were taken out, 'naming and shaming' their target, and Labour MP Gwyn Prosser accused him of 'greed' and 'blatant asset-stripping' in an Early Day Motion.

Buffini's response was to hire a PR – through which we learned that his feet remain very much on the ground, he drinks pints, supports Arsenal and spends his spare time with underprivileged children in poor parts of London fretting about the underachievement of young, often fatherless, black boys. He even launched the charity Private Equity Foundation, although suffered a set-back when the launch event's entertainment featured a semi-clad female pole-dancer. As one guest commented to the *Daily Telegraph*, 'At least they didn't auction the woman off afterwards.'[3]

In the end Buffini agreed to recognize the GMB – although just as the union was preparing the paperwork, they found he was merging the AA with Saga, the over-50s travel and insurance group, in a £6.2 billion deal orchestrated by Permira, CVC and Charterhouse. The merger came with a refinancing deal heaping £4.8 billion of debt on to Saga-AA's balance sheet but offering a nice cash windfall for private equity investors and management. Andrew Goodsell, Saga's chief executive, sent a two-line note to the GMB saying he had no intention of honouring Buffini's recognition.

The GMB's main problem was that there was very little it could do. Private equity companies have no shareholders' meetings the union could attend – hence its lobbying at Buffini's church. There simply is no other access. The advantage with targeting Buffini is that journalists and members of the public at least have some idea who he is. Most of those running private equity funds are entirely anonymous. All funds are constituted as a private company so there is almost no legal responsibility to disclose the ownership structure or corporate behaviour – very different rules than those applying to multi-nationals listed on stock markets around the world. Unlike plcs, firms such as Permira are not governed by stock-market rules regarding openness. They are opaque, secretive organizations only in the business of making money.

According to the University of Manchester's Montgomerie:

> Private equity funds take extreme advantage of the fact that they are set up as limited companies. All their subsidiary funds and investments are set up as holding companies. Then they go out and buy public limited companies – companies with shareholders listed on the stock exchange. Public firms are the benchmark for disclosure. A plc is legally obliged to disclose who's on the board, for instance. They have to disclose directors' remuneration; they have to disclose all kinds of performance data. They have to disclose investments. That's how, for instance,

the environmental lobby can track the behaviour of plcs like BP. The company has to issue information every three months. But the minute a plc is taken over by private equity all of that is hidden – including the amount of debt they're taking on and how they pay themselves. Even if that company, just the year before, was reporting all this information, it vanishes from public scrutiny. What they say is that no limited partnership in the UK is subject to public disclosure – which is true. The corner shop isn't. But these are multi-billion-dollar firms, which are able to say, 'well private means private' – even though they're taking money from municipalities, for example. I think the case for greater transparency in private equity is quite strong. But there has been no movement – only Walker's wonderful voluntary code.

Montgomerie is referring to former Morgan Stanley chairman Sir David Walker's voluntary code – developed at the behest of the British Venture Capital Association – which aimed to head off concerns about secrecy and concealed information. The original consultation document had called for buy-out groups to publish annual reports but Walker's code, published in November 2007, downgraded to an entirely voluntary requirement that their websites be kept up to date with their day-to-day activities. Perhaps understandably, *The Times* said it was 'lacking bite'.

Biteless though the code might be, it was the private equity industry's response to a sudden and very real threat. In June 2007 Nicholas Ferguson, chairman of SVG Capital, let the taper relief cat out of the bag by telling the *Financial Times* that it was odd he paid less tax than his cleaner.[4] The *FT* put the story on the front page and the resulting tabloid fury forced Damon Buffini, Dominic Murphy of Kohlberg Kravis Roberts, Robert

Easton of Carlyle and Philip Yea of 3i, together representing the British Private Equity and Venture Capital Association, to receive a grilling from a Treasury Select Committee a few weeks later. The quartet went to the mother of Parliaments to argue that the tax regime kept the UK competitive. The result was a complete débâcle.

All four evaded questions, specifically how much tax they paid, leading John McFall, the Labour chairman, to scoff, 'You're the masters of the universe. I'm asking how much capital gains tax you pay and you cannot tell me?' Murphy, who was behind the £11 billion takeover of Boots, said that, as a law-abiding citizen, he would pay the level of tax determined by the government, only to reveal that he'd moved to Ireland for tax purposes. Indeed, their lobbying skills were so woeful that MPs publicly sought an excuse for them. McFall, reflecting on Ferguson's cleaner comment, wondered 'Did he just temporarily lose his marbles?'[5]

Such incompetence, however, could not go unpunished. The industry masterminds' fumbling and evasiveness had outraged the committee, and it moved quickly to recommend private equity fund companies be forced to pay a reasonable tax on their billions of pounds' worth of profits. Except, of course, this didn't happen. Instead, the government merely abolished the taper relief exemption they were entitled to and replaced it with a flat 18 per cent fee, then panicked and, in 2008, created entrepreneurs' relief instead – earn up to £750,000 of capital gains on the sale of business assets and you pay only 9 per cent tax.

This seems utterly incomprehensible. The private equity industry, to make this clear, borrows other people's money to buy perfectly healthy companies, then sacks their employees and breaks them up before selling them on at a huge profit. For this they were entitled to tax breaks so vast that the head of one company paid less tax than his cleaner. How did Gordon

Brown, a Labour chancellor committed to ending child poverty, oversee this system? How, when the bosses of these companies behaved like the Marx Brothers in front of our elected representatives, did they get away with – in some cases – a tax cut?

Here was an industry flagrantly stretching taxation rules to breaking point, an industry that intrinsically creates unemployment and refuses to release information on its owners, which, after effectively telling the Treasury it didn't care, got off with an 8 per cent tax hike on earnings over £1 million. According to Montgomerie:

> By all political science accounts there's no way the private equity industry should have done so well in that Treasury Select Committee. They gave a really poor performance, they got hammered by the Select Committee and yet nothing much came of it. We tried to look at some of the reasons why but we couldn't get any understanding.

Even Minister for the City Paul Myners wrote to the *New Statesman* saying,

> Private equity . . . is almost entirely a function of exploiting tax breaks on interest payments . . . employees of private-equity-owned companies get no additional reward for the increased risk attached to their employment. And yet employees will, in some cases, pay the price for this reduced security through loss of jobs or reduction in pensions. One in six of all private sector employees now works in a private-equity-financed business, and even more are exposed, if you count suppliers or customers.[6]

It may be worth flicking back to the list of political party donors at the beginning of this chapter and spend some time reflecting on the curious incident of the committee in the night-time. Then, with those names in mind and the resulting tax rate, look at figures from the Electoral Commission for party donations in the second quarter of 2009.

The total amount donated was up 45 per cent from the first quarter despite the astonishing depth of the downturn. Donations to the Conservative Party increased from £4.3 million to £6.4 million, Labour's increased from £2.8 million to £4.4 million and the Liberal Democrats' was up from £826,751 to £1.1 million. This included a £106,500 donation to the Conservative Party by Michael Hintze, senior investment officer at asset management group CQS, taking his total donations to the party past the £1 million mark. Nigel Doughty, chairman and founder of private equity firm Doughty Hanson, took his total donations to the Labour Party beyond £1.5 million with a £250,000 donation. Crispin Odey, founder of Odey Asset Management, provided £15,000 to the Tories and there were healthy sums given to the party by financier David Rowland, hedge fund manager Michael Farmer and Michael Spencer, who runs investment fund IPGL.[7] What on earth is going on?

John Plender, *Financial Times* columnist, comments on this furtive hand-holding between big City powerbrokers and the government:

> You can see [the power of the City's political influence] in the intellectual battleground about re-regulation. What are we to do about banks that are too big to fail? The crisis has created more powerful superbanks whose very size indicates that they will not be allowed to fail in any future crisis. It's an implicit underwriting of their activities by any future government. The only way to avoid that is to break the banks up. Of course the banks argue against that and they are winning. The odd voice is raised suggesting

a penalizing taxation system but these are largely ignored. The fact that the banks are winning is down to their lobbying power and funding of the political establishment. If you replace the word bank in what I'm saying with Russian oil barons you'll see how effectively the financial elites have reduced us to Third World corruption levels.

Still, at least the private equity industry is just a shadowy group of super-rich individuals, with uncomfortably close ties to democratically elected politicians, who tear British companies apart and rip out cash while avoiding any long-term investment or job creation and have no legal responsibility to give out any information on their activities or pay any significant level of tax for the right to do so. It could be worse. They could be Philip Green.

CHAPTER NINE

IN WHICH PHILIP GREEN COULDN'T
GIVE A FUCK

Around the time Sir Philip Green was working on plans to bid
for Safeway in early 2003, the *Guardian* journalist Ian Griffiths
looked at information filed at Companies House to see if Green's
Bhs business was worth the £1 billion necessary for the bid.
Griffiths had some queries and, in March 2003, called Green to
tell him about the article as well as to ask for responses to a few
questions. What followed, according to Griffiths, who recorded
the phone calls, were three days of 'anger, shouting, abuse and
threats of litigation'. Substantial parts of the conversation were
subsequently published by the *Guardian*:

> Sir Philip Green (PG): 'You are really gonna try my
> patience, you know that?'
> *Guardian*: 'Well, I quite understand . . .'
> PG: 'I've got two bankers on my fucking board . . .'
> *Guardian*: 'Right.'
> PG: 'American director of Barclays fucking Capital,
> Chris Coles, and Robin Saunders, together with Allan
> Leighton as my chairman. But the profits are ficti-
> tious? Sober up!'

Guardian: 'We are not suggesting that the profits are fictitious.'
PG: 'You are!'
Guardian: 'No we are not.'

Later:

PG: 'Is this the *Beano* or the *Guardian*? Shall I tell you something? You know what the shame is? If the laws of this country were like America, right? I'd love you to print that because I'd be able to close you down, put you out of your misery. I've never read a bigger load of bollocks in my life. I've never read such – I'm gonna send this to my lawyers, because it is laughable.'
Guardian: 'In what way?'
PG: 'You don't know what the fuck you are reading. And nor does this Ian Griffiths. You want to fucking sack him. You haven't got a fucking clue. Do you want some lessons? Get in your car, come to my fucking office . . . You can't read, you people. You shouldn't be allowed to write fucking newspapers.'

Then:

PG: 'For fuck's sake. Jesus Christ. Robin Saunders and Chris Coles are on my board. Allan Leighton is my chairman. I've got a fucking audit committee that I am not on. And Ian Griffiths, some old cunt from the *Independent*, knows more than all those people. Please. Go and write about someone else. Do yourself a favour.'

And again:

PG: 'He [Paul Murphy, financial editor] can't read English. Mind you, he is a fucking Irishman.'

Green's final quote is illuminating:

> PG: 'If you go to my accounts it says in there cash
> generated £143 m[illion]. Does he think I got it out of
> a fucking sack at Christmas? The man [Ian Griffiths]
> can't read.'
> *Guardian*: 'Would you be prepared to talk to him?'
> PG: 'I don't want to have to go through this crap.
> That's why I'm private.'[1]

Stewart Lansley and Andy Forrester charted Green's rise and
fall and rise and fall and rise in *Top Man: How Philip Green
Built His High Street Empire*. Philip Green, they revealed.
was born in 1952 in Croydon, a depressingly concrete suburb
in south London that once housed London's airport and was
consequently bombed to smithereens during the Second World
War. His parents were respectably middle class – something
that sits oddly with his current tough-talking geezer persona.
His father ran a handful of companies servicing the burgeoning
TV market while his mother ran a launderette and one of the
first self-service petrol stations. Eventually they made enough
to move away from Croydon, north to East Finchley – an altogether greener and more cheerful part of suburbia – and sent
nine-year-old Philip to an expensive Jewish boarding school:
Carmel College, near Oxford.

Green was slightly out of his depth from the start. The richest
boys were chauffeured to school at the start of term and the
combination of intense academic pressure and additional reli-
gious and Hebrew lessons didn't exactly appeal.

In 1964, when Green was eleven, his father suffered a massive heart attack and died. According to contemporaries, this
had a significant effect on the boy's behaviour. He became
increasingly unruly – although he still loved and excelled at
sport, especially cricket – and at one point was suspended for

an entire term. He would go home at weekends to help his mother run the garage and gradually making money became his main ambition. In the end, he left school without a single O level and took a job his mother secured for him in the whole-sale shoe trade.

It was the 1960s and fashion was moving from upmarket boutiques on to the high street. Green spent five years running errands for his employers and dealing with buyers at trade fairs before joining the board of his family's small property management company and receiving a business loan of £20,000 – around £150,000 in today's money. He set up his own whole-sale fashion business and struck up a friendship with a London entrepreneur called Gerald Weisfeld who also ran a small chain of shops in Scotland called What Every Woman Wants, shortly to be renamed What Everyone Wants – which Green would later buy out.

Green's wholesale business grew until, in 1981, he made his first big mistake. Convinced that the US trend for designer jeans would spread to the UK he persuaded Joan Collins – fresh from her triumph *The Stud*, an erotic thriller – to lend her name to a line of denim. She'd act as the public face and receive royalties on every pair sold. The launch was a disaster, the stock had to be heavily discounted and the following year Green had to wind his company up.

The early-1980s recession, however, proved something of an opportunity. He started buying up high-end boutiques on the verge of closure, taking over their stock and either selling it on or shifting it off the original premises at a huge discount. He also started sourcing designer labels like Armani, Dior and Yves Saint Laurent – which had specific relationships with selected UK stores – from unofficial sources in Europe. The labels and their established stores moved quickly to close loopholes and eventually the stores closed down.

The man, however, was nothing short of irrepressible. In a series of deals, he rescued a distressed jeans company called Bonanza, bought out one of its biggest debtors – the denim chain store Jean Jeanie – and sold the lot to Lee Cooper jeans, where he was appointed managing director of a new division in 1986.

Initially, everything went well. He liked living large – a friend said his weakness was 'slow horses and fast women',[2] after a series of racehorses, such as the appropriately named Bonanza Boy (which went on to win the Welsh Grand National in 1989 after he sold his stake), seriously underperformed during his ownership. He met the woman who would become his wife and he was making powerful new friends among a coterie of Spurs-supporting businessmen like banker Edward Ball, Spurs chairman Irving Scholar, video entrepreneur Stephen Kay and temping agency Blue Arrow's founder Tony Berry.

But corporate culture didn't suit him. He rapidly fell out with the Lee Cooper board and resigned as MD in 1987, halfway into his three-year contract – his third failed attempt to hit the big time in ten years. This time round, however, he had wealthy and influential friends. As the stock market crashed in October 1987, Green seized his chance and put together a bid for 29 per cent of Amber Day – a fashion retail holding company that owned, among other outlets, Kensington's hip boutique Biba and Review, an upmarket men's chain.

To buy the necessary shares, Green borrowed heavily from Kay and Berry as well as stumping up an unspecified amount of his own cash – an amount he later claimed to be £3 million and certainly enough to give him a personal holding of 17 per cent – as well as the roles of chairman and chief executive. Seeing Review as the future, he started an aggressive expansion plan – aiming to rival the likes of Burton with a store on every high street. He snapped up one of Review's competitors – the Woodhouse Group – with a £1 million bid financed by a rights issue of Amber Day shares. He also started to create the now familiar Philip Green legend, buying a flashy house in Marbella, a speedboat and a new London house, as well as courting journalists and bankers with lavish parties and personal phone calls – circumventing Amber Day's more traditional stockbrokers Laing and Cruikshank, who resigned.

As Green talked the talk, rumours of his next takeover targets circulated wildly – in 1989 he made two formal and unsuccessful bids for dickie-bow-and-tux tailors Moss Bros and, so word had it, was looking at Next or even the mighty Sears Group, the US department store giant that owned Selfridges on London's Oxford Street. The City waited with bated breath, aware that profits were falling at Review and Woodhouse as the recession bit.

When Green did move, however, it was a completely different kind of deal – not upmarket, not tailors and not a cunningly wrought lightning bid. In 1990, he agreed to buy the 37 stores that made up Gerald Weisfeld's What Everyone Wants (WEW) chain.

In recent years it's become part of every fashion magazine's mantra that twinning high-end glamour items with quick turnaround, cheaply made couture copies at the likes of Topshop and Primark is not just acceptable but admirable. In 2006, *Vogue* editor Alexandra Shulman gave this tactic the fashionista's seal of approval with the following piece in the *Daily Mail*:

> Friday lunchtime, and the *Vogue* office near Oxford Circus is deserted. Soon most of the girls who work with me will be back at their desks, and most of them will be carrying a carrier bag from one the local High Street stores – Topshop, H&M, Warehouse, New Look.

Payday tends to go together with a hit-and-run raid on the shops, and never more so than now when there is such a huge amount of cheap fashion to satisfy everybody's instant shopping cravings.

For about £30, you can have a new outfit for Saturday night's party – if it gets trashed at that price, who cares.

So cheap are their clothes and so fast their turnover that you can recharge your wardrobe on a weekly basis along-side that of your husband and your children.[3]

When Kate Moss designed a line of clothes for Topshop, police had to be called in to control the crowds on opening day. Newspapers breathlessly reported this phenomenon as unprecedented. In fact, of course, it was nothing of the sort. At WEW in the 1980s, for instance, Weisfeld employed similar tactics. He'd buy cheaply at the end of a fashion season, open large stores near but not actually in expensive shopping centres and, through a blend of cheap stock and cunning marketing, would draw such crowds that when a new shop opened he would regularly have to call the police to control them. Perhaps that's where Green learned his retail skills. Certainly, WEW had increased turnover every year since it launched and had a knack of tying up canny deals during the recession. Philip Green was soon to change that.

Initially, Amber Day's takeover allowed WEW some autonomy – the Weisfelds still owned 17 per cent of their busi-ness. Gerald was even best man at Philip's wedding to Tina in 1990. As Green insisted on carrying through his business ideas, however, the friendship crumbled. A plan to raise prices across the chain and 'make the business sweat', in Weisfeld's words, proved too much for Gerry. The Weisfelds sold their shares and broke off relations with Green in 1991. Shortly afterwards, Green launched a huge and successful rights issue to wipe out the company's debt and appointed two new directors to please the City – Graham Coles as finance director and former Lloyds director Leslie Warman as non-exec. By the end of the year, Amber Day shares were the best-performing quoted share of the year. Green had a good Christmas and, early in the new year, set off on one of his favourite jaunts – heading out to suppliers in the Far East to push their prices down still further.

On Monday 13 January 1992, however, Amber Day's share price started to slide – and it went on falling, almost halving by the end of the month. Initially Amber Day's PR machine blamed short-selling City traders for driving the price down: spreading a few rumours about the financial health of the company – despite being illegal – would have helped bring prices tumbling. And there is certainly evidence to support this claim – some newspapers were on the receiving end of badly disguised fake rumours aimed at undermining the company.

As the year unfolded, however, it became clear that there were problems at Amber Day. After disputes about the make-up of the board, Coles and Warman left the company in June. Warman's resignation was the more damaging. He had been pushing for the appointment of a second independent non-executive director since his arrival and felt Green's joint role as chairman and chief executive would make this less likely. At the company's June board meeting he proposed splitting the roles, lost the vote and quit. The City was uneasy and there was talk of at least an informal inquiry. Green subsequently conceded the need for an independent chairman but the share price kept on falling – by June it had reached 58p, quite some distance from January's 107p.

In July, Green predicted profits of £10 million for Amber Day's financial year. Over August, scandalous stories about some of Green's business friends – including claims that many of them had lent him money to buy his stake in Amber

Day – surfaced, pushing the share price down still further. When September saw profits of £7.5 million – 30 per cent below Green's predictions – institutional shareholders started to abandon ship – beginning with the Prudential. Green resigned.

Says one long-term business associate:

> The Amber Day and the City thing still really, really bugs him, it still really winds him up even today. That's when he switched. He was never going to go back to the City on their terms. Everything was going to be structured finance, using various financial vehicles, buying stuff cheap and stripping out the value to pay for the deal. Take a look at the Bhs deal he did a few years later. When he bought Bhs he paid £200 million. The value of the company's property assets alone was closer to £400 million – but the company was valued off its P/E [profit:earnings] ratio – profits of £20 million give a P/E of 10 gives a price of £200 million.

Even though the humiliation infuriated Green, the incident wasn't a complete disaster. He secured a £1.1 million pay-off, sold his shares a few months later for £7.6 million and, in 1993, used the money to buy Parker & Franks, a fashion chain that had fallen into administration, and relaunched it as a chain of mini-department stores called Xception. He followed this up with a deal to buy the UK's fifth largest chain of full-sized department stores – Owen & Owen, at that time owned by Swedish venture capitalists. He made all the right noises about developing the business but, barely a year after the purchase, sold off eight of the 13 stores to wipe out the company's debt. In 1995 he bought a subsidiary of Bhs called One Up and – within weeks – resold the stores at a handsome profit to Primark.

This was the beginning of the new Green – the deal-maker and buy-out king. The old 'setting up and running a business' side of things had ended in repeated failure – but mainly the running the business bit of it. He'd never had problems buying chains or raising money. Now he began to concentrate on that side of things, starting a new relationship with the City – but never again venturing into the glaring light focused on the plc.

Around the same time as the One Up deal, a banker approached Green to help with Hill Samuel – an ailing jewellery business with shoe chain Foothold attached. Green and fellow entrepreneur Stephen Kay paid off £6 million in debts for the company and thus acquired both the debt and 15 per cent of the shares. Using the debt as a bargaining tool – he could, at any time, have put the company into liquidation as its assets were considerably less than £6 million – he forced the other shareholders to close down Hill Samuel and sell off Foothold and leave him with a tidy profit.

Before the year was out, Green would pull off one more coup. A young Scottish entrepreneur called Tom Hunter approached him for help buying the Olympus Sports shops chain. Olympus was haemorrhaging money for its owner – the vast Sears empire, which also owned Miss Selfridge and Warehouse – but the group didn't take 34-year-old Hunter seriously as a buyer. Although he'd built up the rival Sports Division chain from nothing, he could still raise only some £12 million. Green – and a corporate finance whizz-kid at the Bank of Scotland called Peter Cummings – pulled together £20 million and persuaded Sears to part with Olympus. Within a year Hunter was turning a profit; within two years – Green slowed down for a while post-Olympus after chest pains and a heart attack scare then re-entered the game – Green had started sniffing around Sears itself.

The retail behemoth was struggling against leaner, fitter rivals and its shareholders were getting restless as a deal with Littlewoods to sell catalogue company Freemans and with

Facia group to take on shoe shops Saxone and Curtess ended in disaster. In 1997 a liquidator was appointed to break up the Sears group. Green tied up a deal to buy most of the shops in yet another Sears footwear chain, Shoe Express, which had a property portfolio that largely complemented that of Mark One – a women's fashion chain he'd added to his growing portfolio in February 1996. He swiftly rebranded half of the Shoe Express stores – at a stroke expanding Mark One by 75 stores – and sold the remaining stores for more than double the entire amount he'd laid out.

In 1998 Green moved to Monaco – ostensibly for his health. He bought an £8 million hilltop penthouse apartment overlooking the sea. His Gulfstream G550 rests on Nice airport's tarmac while he's in town, and his 206-foot (63-metre) Benetti – which cost around £20 million – lies in Monaco harbour alongside the equally large *Lady Beatrice*, owned by the semi-retired Barclay brothers.

Says the business associate:

> I know someone who'd worked with Green on a couple of deals and had just sold his company. They were on the phone and Green said, 'How much did you get?' The guy said £30 million. Green said, 'I'd get more than that for one of my Ribs.' That's a rigid-hulled inflatable boat – the boat that takes him to his £180 million yacht. That's the way he operates. His yacht tenders cost £30 million.

Having met in Monte Carlo, the Barclay brothers and Green prepared a little wager back in London, preparing a takeover vehicle called January Investments, which combined Green and Hunter's money with some £100 million from the Barclays. They swooped on Sears in January 1999, paying £548 million, selling it off chunk by chunk for a total of £800 million. In 2000 he bought Bhs for £200 million, adding the Arcadia Group – owners of Topshop, Burton, Miss Selfridge and Dorothy Perkins – in 2002 (the Safeway bid never did come to fruition. In October 2003 he finally declined to bid.) He managed all of this without the need for shareholder scrutiny or, now he lived in Monaco and had restructured his business around his wife, paying any tax.

In 2005, for instance, Green banked £1.2 billion after awarding himself the biggest pay cheque in British corporate history. The huge dividend was more than four times Arcadia's pre-tax profits of £253 million and nearly £100 million more than the previous record, held by Lakshmi Mittal, who paid himself £1.1 billion after merging Ispat and LNM Holdings. Green's £1.2 billion, however, was paid to Tina, officially resident in Monaco and the direct owner of Arcadia, and thus tax-free.

Says analyst Matthew Lynn:

> Philip Green won't work through a listed company for obvious reasons – too much accountability. He ships all his money offshore without paying any tax in a completely outrageous way. Nobody touches his tax status, [and yet he's] almost entirely funded by Halifax/Bank of Scotland. He couldn't have risen to where he is without HBOS funnelling [him] millions of pounds. Why is that so different from one of the Russian oligarchs? He has Topshop selling us cheap dresses because we don't have oil, we have high streets.

This set-up first came to the public's attention during Green's unsuccessful attempt to buy Marks & Spencer in 2000. After backroom machinations, rumour and counter-rumour, lawyers demanded all potential players reveal their hands. A surprised retail industry found Philip didn't have any stock in M&S, but Tina had snaffled 9.5 million of M&S's shares for £23 million through offshore accounts in the Channel Islands – just before her husband announced his interest in the company. Although entirely legal, it didn't seem so to lawyers and journalists at the time and it further alarmed City elders who hired Kroll Associates to look into Green's business practices.

The situation didn't endear bankers to him. Says an ex-banker:

Doing deals with him can be frightening. He's got a sign on the wall of his office that says 'Good morning . . . Let the stress begin'. He always has three phones on the go – certain people have certain numbers and I don't think any of them are for personal calls. He's always on the phone – always. People who've been in meetings one-on-one with him say he's as nice as pie when you walk in. He sits on his big chair with his legs crossed – swearing all the time, fuck this, fuck that, but very laid back. As soon as you cross the line of business though, his eyes roll back in his head, his neck spins round and it's like a shark attack. All that foreplay and after that he doesn't care if you're enjoying it or not – he's going to fuck you.

I was at one meeting when there were around 16 people in the room, eight from each side of the deal. He was late – the last one there – and he walked in, sat down and took a call. He was taking calls all the way through the meeting and if he wasn't on the phone he'd be looking at them. One poor bloke from Barclays, who wasn't working for Green, tried to raise this point about value and rentals and Green just said, 'Who the fuck are you? I want solutions not problems. You're not even on my side. Get out of the room.' The bloke had all these files in front of him – he was pretty senior. Everyone else was staring at their shoes. The meeting carried on for a minute or so then Green stopped it. The guy had to pick up all his folders and leave. At that point, of course, he'd [Green] won absolute control of the room. He does it [behaves like this] to smack people down, to get control.

Green still needed bankers though. Merrill Lynch helped put together the finance to buy Topshop, with HBOS stumping up most of the money after Green's initial partner – the Icelandic retail chain Baugur – was raided by the Icelandic fraud squad. The deal – in 2002 – marked Green's gradual move from the business pages to the gossip columns, where his lunches were covered with the kind of awed glee normally reserved for pop stars and actors:

'Naomi Campbell trying to muscle in on Kate Moss' territory?!' read a headline on gossip website Mr Paparazzi in August 2009, the article noting:

Yesterday we caught up with the supermodel in Formentera where she was hanging out with Topshop boss Sir Phil Green. Billionaire Philip Green – who's a close pal of Mossy's – took Naomi and her boyfriend Vladislav Doronin to lunch before inviting the pair back to his yacht for a sunbathe. So do you reckon a Naomi Campbell Topshop range could be in the works? Oh Kate Moss would love that, wouldn't she?!

Green's millionaire status, and the press coverage it attracted, didn't happen overnight, of course. His first move on buying Arcadia in 2002 was, obviously, to make redundancies and force suppliers' prices down. Then he withdrew from the pricey Ethical Trading Initiative, which tried to ensure good working conditions around the world, and finally he encouraged the chains to copy Spain's Zara in speeding up their response to the vagaries of fashion.

Zara was founded and is owned by Spain's richest man, Amancio Ortega Gaona, who in 1984 developed a production and distribution system that allowed clothing to go from drawing board to shop floor in as little as ten days. In its Spanish home town of La Coruña, Zara's design team works in large halls – one for women's wear, one for men's wear and one for children's clothes – with floor-to-ceiling windows overlooking the countryside. Hand-held computers lock into the central ordering system, so that if a shop in west London runs out of an item, the manager can order more or suggest alterations, and the designers see the request at the same time as Ortega. Shop managers are trusted to know their catchment area and have the freedom to choose stock to suit their clientele.

Green's Arcadia chains and his Bhs stores changed their mode of operation, relying on quick turnaround fashion – but Green took it one better by hiring designers like Christopher Kane, Stella Vine and Todd Lynn to create collections at high street prices.

Hitting the high street fashion button also seems to have pepped up Green's already flourishing social life. His parties soon began to rival the Mittals' wedding in opulence and splendour. The national media reported his 50th birthday in 2002 with breathless glee as he flew 200 revellers to Cyprus for private performances from Tom Jones and Rod Stewart. At a toga party on the final day, he dressed as Emperor Nero, and Tina gave him a solid gold Monopoly set featuring his own acquisitions. Three years later, he spent £4 million on his 13-year-old son's bar mitzvah in the south of France. But his 55th birthday party in May 2007 topped the lot at a cool £6 million. In a bid to keep the location secret, 200 friends – including

Allan Leighton, chairman of the Royal Mail Group, Richard Desmond, owner of Express Newspapers, Bill Kenwright, the theatre director and impresario, Jilly Johnson, the former Page 3 girl, Eddie Jordan, the Formula 1 boss, and Charles Dunstone, the Carphone Warehouse owner – were sent a 'travel wallet' containing instructions to pack shorts and turn up at Stanstead airport prepared for a long flight. They flew into Soneva Fushi, a luxury spa resort on the island of Kunfunadhoo in the Maldives, for a five-day celebration that culminated in a private concert by George Michael, Jennifer Lopez and Ricky Martin.

Shortly before his 55th birthday, Green received an unlikely early present from Gordon Brown – a knighthood. Unlikely for many reasons, but chiefly because of his sustained policy of avoiding paying tax to the country of the monarch he would receive the honour from. As Nick Cohen wrote in the *Observer*:

> . . . in the spring, the BBC's *Money Programme* calculated that Green and his family had 'saved themselves' £300m from their £1.2bn salary by living for a part of the year in Monaco, whose residents don't pay income tax.
>
> Of course, one person's tax break is another person's tax burden. The £300m the Green family 'saved themselves' must be paid by people who earn considerably less than £1.2bn a year or £1.2m a year or even £120,000 a year.
>
> Standing up for such paupers used to be the point of a Labour government. Even if it could not force the likes of Green to pay their fair share, it retained the power to shun them and make it clear that those who don't contribute towards their country can't expect their country to be grateful.
>
> Even that modest defiance of the plutocrats is beyond Labour now. Yesterday, the Queen announced her birthday

honours and high on her list was Green, who received a
knighthood for 'services to the retail industry'.

If I were in the Inland Revenue, I would fret about the
moment when the little people who stupidly still pay taxes
realise that the state is treating them like fools. It insists that
they must hand over their earnings on pain of punishment
by the courts, while inviting Philip Green to Buckingham
Palace to be honoured by the Queen.[4]

It is not clear why Green – ultimately the largest private equity
operator in the UK – came in for special favours from Brown
although he does have a friendly relationship with the party. In
2003 he paid £18,000 for a game of tennis with Tony Blair.[5] On
13 July 2006, Lord Levy, the chief political fundraiser for the
Labour Party, was arrested by police investigating the 'cash for
peerages' scandal just as he was preparing to meet Lord Adonis
and Sir Philip Green, although Green insists, 'I don't do politics, as such.'[6]

Only stumping up for a tennis game with Tony Blair and
arranging to meet Labour Party fundraisers doesn't seem to
have hurt and the knighthood was certainly not the last favour
he received – there's Brown's tax breaks on all private equity
deals, the complex corporate structures that allow Green to
pay no tax whatsoever and a deal with a government-funded
Fashion Retail Academy north of Oxford Street that supplies him with endless interns.[7] In March 2009, just before
Green announced Topshop's push into the US, the Prime
Minister's wife Sarah Brown personally gave gifts from the
high street chain to President Obama's daughters Malia and
Sasha. Sweet.

Within months of his Buckingham Palace investiture, Green
signed a deal with Kate Moss, rumoured to have netted the
store in excess of £40 million in sales – just when scandal

seemed to have tainted the model for ever. 'The Kate Moss deal was genius,' says Green's business associate. 'She gets caught sniffing coke and H&M drop her like a stone. Green says, come on over and design your own line. He knows every girl on the high street wants to be Kate Moss.'

Piling it high and selling it cheap isn't such a straightforward game these days, however. In November 2005 a man dressed as a green Father Christmas, and carrying a sack of letters about inhuman working conditions in developing world factories tried to deliver the sack to the Topshop at London's Oxford Circus. Security guards turned him away. Two weeks later a full demonstration – with placards, leaflets and chanting – besieged the same store while Green was paying a visit.[8]

Aware that the mood on the high street might be changing, he gave three ethical clothing lines – People Tree, Hug and Gossypium – concessions in the Oxford Street store. Immediately afterwards, however, other ethical trading groups targeted Green for pulling out of the Fair Trade Initiative. An investigation revealed that supplies for Bhs, Wallis and Dorothy Perkins came from one of the sweatshops with the worst reputation – the Fortune Garment & Woolen Knitting Factory in Cambodia.

These ethical protests won't go away. In March 2009 War on Want organized a national protest against Topshop, picketing Topshop locations throughout the country and targeting students – a key demographic among its customers – to boycott the store because of its exploitation of workers. 'The 1.2 billion dividend for Sir Philip Green, who owns UK retailer Topshop, was enough to double the salaries of Cambodia's whole garment workforce for eight years,' its leaflet read.

Green, of course, has no shareholders' meeting that protesters can attend so has no need to enter dialogue unless sales start to fall significantly. Indeed, his moves of supplier have all been about cutting costs – money which, because his firm is private, goes straight into his pocket. He can run his firm for long-term gain or short-term cash.

In 2004 his complex games with the press, with shareholders and with cash failed to secure him Marks & Spencer for the second time of asking. In October he announced Arcadia's impressive results – pre-tax profits up 30 per cent to £246 million – which he had no legal obligation to do. It was partly ego, but mainly to demonstrate to the following day's M&S shareholders' meeting that they should have gone with him. If M&S had gone into Green's empire, he claims he would have kept it listed. Former colleagues and business associates doubt it. Green's ex-banker explains:

> There's a level of money that just moves in the stratosphere. He's worth, what, £4.5 billion? He's got the ability to change the price of the market. He's got various structured finance vehicles, people putting stuff out there for him. The analogy would be like *The Wire*. People like Philip Green and Mike Ashley [the Sports Direct tycoon] are the Stringer Bells. They're the players of the game. The City is like the police. They'd like to know what's going on but they aren't in the game at all – they've got this shareholder democracy to report back to. The people with the big money don't have the same rules as the ones governing the City. They're effectively lawless.

'I don't really know why he keeps going,' the banker, who left the City when he'd made enough to live comfortably for a few years, comments.

> He's horribly driven – even his long-serving staff, his mates, once they're out they don't want to go back. The

thing is, no matter how long you're with him, you're only ever an adviser. You're very well paid, but you're only an adviser. One guy I know who looked after things for him at Arcadia had been with him for a number of years – he did one last deal just after he hit 50 and then he left. He said, 'I'm bored with being kicked in the same places. I'm 55, I've built a new boat and I've got a new wife. Why stick my head in the lion's mouth again?'

In July 2009, Green announced plans to merge Bhs and his Arcadia stores into one business to save money on shop rental. Evans, Burton, Wallis and Dorothy Perkins had been tested in Bhs stores and he was happy with the results. He expected the combined revenues would be around £3 billion a year. He told journalists that he also wants to launch Topshop in Paris, Milan and China. 'This will probably make us the largest private player in the UK with 44,000 people', he added,[9] stressing the private as he had done when yelling at the *Guardian*.

The irony is that while we, the citizens, are under increasing surveillance, the companies that employ us and do business with us have become increasingly opaque. In February 2009, the House of Lords – not exactly a body one typically associates with worrying about public privacy – said British people are now spied on to the same degree as the citizens of the average dictatorship. Monitoring of our lives has become 'pervasive' and 'routine', they warned. Every day an astonishing range of information is gathered, extending from phone calls, internet usage and e-mails to the Oyster cards used on London's transport system and store loyalty cards.

And yet, Philip Green represents the opposite trend – the movement of money and the power-wielding of big business into the shadows. According to Karel Williams of Manchester University's Centre for Research on Socio-Cultural Change, the economic crisis in Britain during the 1970s produced profound changes in the political economy 'but their chief political function was to insulate markets from the influence of democratic government'.

Bloomberg analyst Matthew Lynn fears the consequences of this trend:

> In France, the super-elite are known as the enarques, from the Ecole Nationale d'Administration [ENA], which is basically where the French elite are educated. There are 90 students a year and if you graduate you go anywhere from the board of Havas to the Mayor of Lille. It's all very smooth and very rigid. The country is run by the enarques and that's 100 people a year. You either get into ENA and you're part of the ruling elite or you don't and you don't really count. That's why they have riots all the time because the ruling elite don't listen to the middle classes – voting doesn't make much difference so you have to get out on the streets with Molotov cocktails. That's the risk we have in the UK. We used to know where the power lay and we could influence it in some way but now it's all behind closed doors.

This all sounds a little too much like the final chapter of *Animal Farm*, where the farm animals stare in though a window at a dozen farmers and half a dozen of the more eminent pigs, drinking a toast together and failing to notice those on the outside looking at them. We are the animals, gazing through the glass as the politicians and the oligarchs drink together. We look from pig to man, and from man to pig, and from pig to man again; but already it is impossible to say which is which.

Although perhaps that analogy is unfair. At least the pigs let the animals look through the windows. Here, the cameras are turned on us, while the charity balls and tax breaks and knighthoods and donations and legislation loopholes and invitations and opaque debt trading and bailouts and lay-offs and all the rest take place behind closed doors and on newly invisible balance sheets. It's no longer a question of what's best for the economy – it's become how best can we defend democracy.

CHAPTER 10

IN WHICH WE TRY TO LEND A HELPING HAND

In November 2009, John Cassidy, author of *How Markets Fail*, gave a lecture at the London School of Economics in which he tried to understand the causes of the global crash. The problem had begun, he argued, with the collapse of the post-war idea that government had any part to play in the market – meaning those who believed in the social purpose of government and the market had effectively abandoned the field of economics to the libertarian inheritors of Adam Smith's ideas.

Smith argued that the market operates as an 'invisible hand', righting all wrongs through its innate perfection. 'It is not from the benevolence of the butcher, the brewer or the baker, that we expect our dinner, but from their regard to their own self-interest,' Smith's most famous quotation begins. 'We address ourselves, not to their humanity but to their self-love, and never talk to them of our own necessities but of their advantages.'

This pursuit of self-interest, thought Smith, drives the market to self-regulate. Every monopoly or excessively high price will create its own gravedigger in the form of an eager, light-footed competitor. Government's responsibility regarding cartels, monopolies and the like – which, it is fair to say although Smith didn't, includes oligarchs and cabals of lobbyists – was simply to stop encouraging them. It should not intervene; the market would correct itself.

For the group of academics known as the Chicago School – a term coined in the 1950s to refer to academics who gathered together at the University of Chicago's school of business at the height of Keynesianism to plot the downfall of its interventionist brand of economics – what Cassidy had to say was simply babble from a soft-hearted liberal. Still influential today, in the late twentieth century the Chicago School created the ideas that set up our globalized world and led to the recent crash. Home to the likes of Milton Friedman, the great popularizer of free market economics, who strongly advocated monetarism as an instrument of government policy, and Eugene Fama, creator of the efficient-market hypothesis, now Professor of Finance at Chicago, the Chicago School also attracted fellow-travellers such as the economist Friedrich von Hayek, who believed 'social justice is an empty phrase with no determinable content'. In 1978, von Hayek argued, in a letter to *The Times*, that if Margaret Thatcher said

> free choice is to be exercised more in the market place than in the ballot box . . . she has merely uttered the truism that the first is indispensable for individual freedom while the second is not: free choice can at least exist under a dictatorship that can limit itself but not under the government of an unlimited democracy which cannot.

If anyone was unsure of his meaning, he made it plain to a journalist from the Chilean newspaper *El Mercurio* when visiting and praising Augusto Pinochet in 1981: 'Personally I prefer a liberal dictator to democratic government lacking liberalism.' He went on to suggest Pinochet could teach the UK a thing or two and thus won the Nobel Prize, a knighthood and the Presidential Medal of Freedom – which must have referred to a very specific kind of freedom under which torture and death squads are to be highly recommended.

Von Hayek's influence over Friedman was profound – and not just in their shared admiration of, encouraging visits to, and suggesting policies for, Pinochet's Chile. Friedman created monetarism in his mentor's image – the economic and political theory which opposed central banks, government intervention, regulation and pretty much everything other than moves to control inflation. Along the way he devised the premise that rational consumers would spend a proportional amount of what they perceived to be their permanent income while the rest and any windfall gains would mostly be saved. Hence, he argued, tax reductions would likewise be saved, as rational consumers would predict that taxes would have to increase later to balance public finances. Bless him.

Fama, an altogether more pedestrian economist, has no dictators under his belt but holds a firm belief that markets – in particular stock markets – 'know' everything they need to know, that all the information available is reflected in prices and thus they are perfectly efficient. You can't buck the market.

These ideas came to the fore in the 1970s, as Keynesianism's dream of a consensus society rotted under the mounds of un-collected rubbish in London's Leicester Square. Through think tanks, lobbying bodies and factions within the Conservative and Republican parties these theorists fought long and hard to inflict the worship of an entirely unrestrained free market on the world via the good offices of Western governments and the IMF.

For its opponents, the wealth of the West at the end of the 1980s was hypnotizing, and within a decade Chubais in Russia,

Deng in China, Collor in Brazil and Singh in India had created their own local imitations. The promise of the vast changes that followed, and shook the world in the early 1990s as these and other countries sought to mirror the West's success, was tantalizing – the oppressive brutality of communist regimes swept away, the end of apartheid and a wave of social change in South America and the Indian subcontinent.

It would clearly be crazy to bite the invisible hand – trade globalization and freer markets have given millions of people far more than the vicious inequalities of the Soviet Union. And yet, paradoxically, blind faith in a faultless market has produced such huge inequality itself that even the party that brought this philosophy to the UK seems appalled at the horrors it has wrought.

In November 2009, a high-ranking Tory adviser, Philip Blond – hailed without any apparent irony as party leader David Cameron's 'Philosopher King' – launched a harsh critique of 'cartel-driven capitalism'. The ideology of the 1980s quashed public morality, created 'a casino economy', globalization without competition, wealth without fairness and 'state-sanctioned monopoly capitalism'.[1] Blond was speaking to attract UK voters, so he didn't take the next step and point to the astonishing consequence of this bleak, cold and carelessly vicious market – that it removed so many of the old certainties that some people actually yearn for a return to the misery of dictatorship.

Take the unfortunate people of Seboken Hostels near the Vanderbjlpark steel mill. Under the old apartheid system, factories recruited workers from as wide a variety of locations as possible, to avoid employing large groups of men with strong regional ties. They built hostels on-site or next door to the factories, mines and mills where their employees could sleep. Sometimes these were no better than a vast dormitory filled with bunks. Sometimes, as in the case of Vanderbjlpark's Seboken Hostels, they look pretty much like a large council estate in the UK – rows of four-storey brick-built flats covering a couple of miles and housing around 6,800 single men and families.

In 2001, as Lakshmi Mittal took control of the day-to-day running of the metal extraction company ISCOR, the company decided to sell off all its housing provision, including Seboken. The agreement was to return the hostels to the control of the local council but one council employee spotted an opportunity. With a couple of friends, he approached the steel company and offered to buy Seboken for R5 million – about R5 million more than the company was expecting from the council. His plan was to sell the homes on to his employer immediately for a cool R15 million: R10 million in the bank – nice job done. Albeit an illegal one. When he tried to sell, however, the council pointed out that it couldn't take part in the deal as there were laws against exactly what he'd just done. The man was left with a sprawling estate, home to almost 7,000 people, that he had no interest in running.

He went to talk to the residents to ask if they would leave their homes as he had a developer interested in buying the place. They refused. He became angry and walked out. A little while later, he uprooted the cable supplying electricity to Seboken, leaving the entire estate with no power. Shortly after that, something happened to the water supply – the pressure dropped significantly, meaning the top three floors of the hostels had no running water. The owner sent word that he was prepared to negotiate the residents' departure. They refused. Again.

In 2002, a group of armed private security guards arrived at Seboken and started forcibly evicting families. Word spread quickly round the estate and almost everyone came running. A pitched battle raged around the buildings for almost an hour – fist fights, rifle fire and baton charges on both sides. At the end of the encounter, four of the security guards were dead. They didn't come back.

Visiting Seboken today is about as bleak as you'd imagine. The residents have dug down to water pipes beneath the ground to create clean springs every few hundred yards, but the water flowing out serves as sewer as well as supply. The snaking rivers of shit-strewn, filthy water winding their way downhill into stagnant pools give off such a foul odour that you gag whenever you have to cross one – balancing precariously on temporary piles of brick that serve as stepping-stones.

Often the stench is mercifully blocked by the scent of wood smoke – with no electric power, most people cook over open fires. Some enterprising residents have run cables to nearby power lines, effectively pirating an electricity supply. You can see the flimsy cables above your head as you walk, looking a little like clothes lines, stretching from the windows. The cables are hard to attach, however, and when there are violent storms they break loose and fall to the ground where the current, parti-cularly during heavy rainfall, is strong enough to kill children. Meanwhile, of course, Mittal's children have huge mansions in a private tree-lined avenue in Kensington – paid for by their father.

'I don't see what responsibility we have for Seboken,' Nku Nyembezi-Heita argued in the ArcelorMittal boardroom. 'We sold a property five years ago and now the new landlords aren't behaving well – is that our responsibility?' But was it not the company's responsibility to avoid illegal property deals? Is there no duty of care that needs to be taken when selling the homes of men, women and children who may have moved hun-dreds of miles to work there and had nowhere else to go? Not if social justice is an empty phrase.

The desolation caused by von Hayek's dismissal of social justice isn't simply a developing world issue. In the UK the post-war generation raised on Keynesian economics now look to be our luckiest generation. It's strangely acceptable to pour scorn on the 1970s and to express relief that the sorry days of unions protecting people's jobs, of governments having to organize economic policies around the population's needs, of low crime rates and social mobility are behind us. Yet today, for the first time since 1945, it's no longer possible to assume that future generations will be better off, safer and healthier.

The fear of this future drenches the January 2007 report from the Development, Concepts and Doctrine Centre of the Ministry of Defence 'Global Strategic Trends, 2007–2036'. Highlighting the dangers it saw developing over the next 30 years – global warming and the possibility of abrupt climate change, together with the end of 'the golden age of cheap energy', terrorism, rogue states, and the proliferation of weapons of mass destruction feature – it also foresaw the globalization of the world economy and the re-emergence of great power rivalry as a result of the economic development of the BRIC and other states, the continuing decline of US hegemony, and the 'stagnation' of Europe, embodying 'particularly ruthless laws of supply and demand', and creating 'new interdependencies, contradictions, and conflicts'. The report warns:

> . . . the middle classes could become a revolutionary class, taking the role envisaged for the proletariat by Marx. The globalization of labour markets and reducing levels of national welfare provision and employment could reduce peoples' attachment to particular states. The growing gap between themselves and a small number of highly visible super-rich individuals might fuel disillusion with meritocracy, while the growing urban under-classes are likely to pose an increasing threat to social order and stability,

as the burden of acquired debt and the failure of pension provision begins to bite.

In the 1930s, a global crisis ushered in an era of social welfare, public companies and levelling of inequality. This time round it's different. 'At one level we expected the slump to be followed by the New Deal,' Manchester University's Professor Karel Williams believes, arguing that the crisis actually reinforced government dependency on the wealthy. As well as Prime Minister Gordon Brown's appointments to the 'Business Council for Britain', the Treasury and the Mayor of London commissioned reports from City finance groups about the importance of maintaining the competitiveness of London as an international financial centre. The resulting Bischoff and Wigley reports represented a new kind of politics where finance reports on finance by telling stories about finance. Bischoff group members collectively had 662 years of work experience and 75 per cent of those years were spent in City occupations or servicing City needs. Wigley called expert witnesses but 90 per cent of them came from finance or from consultancies with revenue links to finance.

This is very different from earlier inquiries into finance from, for instance, the Macmillan Committee of 1931 to the Wilson Committee of 1980. These heard multiple points of view, different viewpoints were represented on the committee and the written and oral evidence produced significantly more balanced reports. In the case of Macmillan, dissents, reservations and addenda accounted for one-third of the pages in the final report. Bischoff and Wigley were effectively unanimous.

Karel Williams agrees with the former Conservative political adviser Hywel Williams's book *Britain's Power Elites* when it argues that the City has won all the necessary battles for command and control. Karel Williams goes further, however:

At least in 1929 we had an independent intelligentsia, a strong trade union movement with its own organic intellectuals and the Labour Party representing a broad mass movement. Today Labour membership is 150,000 and falling, the intellectuals are weaker than when they faced Thatcher – at least we had independent economic thought in the 1980s – the trade union movement is marginalized and there is no modern equivalent to Nye Bevan. The only advantage we have today is technology – in the 1980s, if you were up to economic trouble-making you had to carry your papers to the news desks in a brown envelope. Today you can post it on your website.

Williams and his colleagues prepared their own proposals to regulate the City post-crash – which he describes as 'principles for action'. His aim is to increase the accountability and transparency of financial elites. He wants to:

i.   Top-slice the lump of revenue now allocated to senior management [in City finance companies], which currently gives them the right to nearly half of net turnover. Claiming this money, CRESC believes, is politically justifiable because it was elite traders who created the fragile system that failed, and because it recompenses taxpayers for state funds spent on bailing out banks and markets.
ii. Remove risk by simplifying banking and ensuring shorter transaction chains.
iii. Shrink the sector by reversing the long-standing policy bias in favour of finance. Greater transparency is a necessary prerequisite for a more democratic finance. Encourage shrinkage by reducing rather than increasing the flow of feedstock from retail by, for example, preferring graduate tax to student loans.

iv. Introduce a new kind of regulator in retail, broadly advised by a retail banking committee drawing on the expertise of SMEs [Small and Medium Enterprises], trade unions and NGOs. The regulator would have a broad brief to include extending the range of advice available in high street banks and curbing banking business models that are currently too sales-based.[2]

The ideas are unlikely to get much purchase. Speaking at the London School of Economics in September 2009 Philip Augar, former equities broker and author of *The Greed Merchants* and *The Death of Gentlemanly Capitalism*, argued:

> The problem is that the influence of the City, the wealthy and business leaders reaches deep into the heart of pretty much every government – the UK Treasury, for instance, has absolute faith in them. For that to be any different there needs to be a credible alternative to the system we currently have. For instance, part of the problem with superbanks could be [resolved by] . . . break[ing] them up into three classes of bank – high street retail banks which the government would underwrite, trading banks like Goldman Sachs that could be cut loose if they collapse over toxic assets, and advisory banks that provided expertise but couldn't trade. At the moment all three are combined into single banks. No nation state's government has the clout or even the incentive to begin something as small-scale as that. We need to have a complete change in the philosophical and political climate. I think for that to happen we would need another crash – but the next one will be deeper, longer and worse than this one.

The real crisis, in other words, is one of democratic control.

The Thatcher market reforms of the early 1990s didn't release the democratic energy of the masses, they released the economic energy of the elite. This elite is not good at organizing the economy – it's good at trading coupons.

Essentially we have to reassert democratic control over the market – whether that be the dealing rooms of the City or the international expansion of a global oligarch. Hedge funds, tax havens, complex corporate vehicles, private equity – they are anti-democratic. Warren Buffett said you shouldn't invest in something you don't understand. Democratic societies shouldn't allow business practices they don't understand.

It may be that all will be well – that the BRIC countries' economies will democratize, that cronyism will diminish, that private equity funds will relinquish their hold over 20 per cent of the UK's employees and that global oligarchs will join the Robber Barons in preferring charitable endeavour to the machinations of power and money. But at the moment, there's no evidence that will happen and, which is worse, we have no clear way to make it so.

This is not simply an argument from hand-wringing liberals – it's an argument about the course of history. Democracy and capitalism grew up together for essential rather than accidental reasons. The economist Von Hayek's worship of the market came from the luxurious position of post-war America. It was easy to mock the social concerns of the majority because those social concerns were a given. The laws, the nation states, the huge capital bestowed on the market by consumer spending – they all arose from the survival of democracy. Plcs might wish their shareholder meetings were not an opportunity for Greenpeace to jostle and yell, but that pressure is an essential part of the security that allows those same shareholders to invest with confidence. Even the most ardent monetarist must, in the end, bow to the existence of social concerns. But how do we secure them?

The key is in refusing to look back, believes Karel Williams:

> We need an alliance of forces old and new. In the UK and the US trade unions have become marginalized and stupid. Talk of remutualization is really some dream of a golden past – a sentimentalized version of a past that never really existed. It's hard for the new forces like NGOs to separate themselves from talk of shareholder value and old corporate structures. Oxfam and MSF [Médicins sans Frontières] did a pretty good job against GlaxoSmithKlein in sub-Saharan Africa but they are not doing well against the City and the super-rich. We need an intelligible and anchorable story offering a portfolio of actions to provide what the economy needs.

Global Action on ArcelorMittal's Sunita Dubey believes that, where targeting shareholders had success in the past, targeting the oligarchs themselves will have results in the very long term:

> After the ArcelorMittal merger Mr Lakshmi Mittal became conscious that people were talking about his company and its reputation in the world. When we met them for the first time they said all the right things – they said they were serious about stakeholder participation, they believe in sharing information and all the social work is very important for them. And they agreed to some of the things that we were demanding. But when we came back, it became – 'Oh, this is the jurisdiction of the national office and the international office doesn't have control of the national office.' It was a way of hiding. Over the years we

learned our lesson, became smarter and did more ground-work. We are on a learning curve and we will see what is going to happen but our strength lies in our local-level groups who are keeping their eyes on ArcelorMittal's local activities.

Dubey agrees that it must be about alliances. In the past, she argues, the environmental movement has been cavalier in its view of unions and jobs. Today it is not enough to strike without talking to NGOs. It is not enough to seek to shut down power plants without talking to trade unions. It is not enough to run through the City for a couple of hours until kettled by the police. It is not enough to repeat mantras that held true over a hundred years ago but sound like the dead hand of oppression today. We need new ideas and new relationships to deal with anti-democratic financial and economic power whether it lies in the hands of rapacious billionaires or secretive financiers. These super-rich are internationalized beyond any nation states' wildest dreams. They have no nation while we squabble over the racial make-up of our own.

We must protest, but opting for the sporadic smashing of windows of those who seemingly abuse their power is worse than useless. It just allows for another CCTV camera and a new private security force inside their shops or banks. And all the while dubious deals will be going on in back rooms to which we have no access. In December 2009, for instance, environmental lobbying group Sandbag revealed that ArcelorMittal has been given far more carbon permits than it needs – indeed, it has the largest allocation of any organization in Europe. Sandbag had used a freedom of information request to see letters – some written by Lakshmi Mittal himself – in which the company threatened to move plants out of Europe at a cost of 90,000 jobs if it were asked to pay for permits. ArcelorMittal is now free to sell its surplus permits on the market or to hoard them for future use. The latter means it could avoid cutting greenhouse gas emissions for years, undermining the entire point of the scheme.

Business journalist John Cassidy, author of *How Markets Fail*, believes pressure should and can be applied to governments – unconsciously echoing Friends of the Earth's policy that each time you think about doing something to help the environment, whether it be recycling or buying low-energy light bulbs, take time to apply pressure, even if it's something as simple as writing a letter to your MP. The *vox populi* must be heard wherever governments turn. At the moment, their ears are cupped by wealthier hands than ours. We have to shout very loud to be heard.

The principle, however, has already been won – albeit accidentally. Bailing out banks and oligarchs in the crash tears apart the theories of the Chicago School. Unrestrained markets are not the solution. Says Cassidy:

> Once we have accepted that certain markets have externalities – that we cannot afford to let the banks fail as they supply the credit that keeps capitalism working – then we accept that some markets have too much responsibility to be left alone. The market is good at aggregating private benefit and private cost but not good at aggregating social benefit and social cost. The market will not act to prevent global warming unless it is made to do so – by artificial pricing, by taxation or [by] other means.

It has worked in the past. Release of the gas that causes acid rain – sulphur dioxide – has fallen dramatically in the US since 1990's Clean Air Act. This taxed the emission of SO_2, set up a release permit trading system and encouraged capture technologies that created an entire industry. Environmental groups in the States have bought SO_2 release permits to take them off the market, thus reducing the total amount that can be released – the kind of direct action that doesn't involve stapling yourself to a tree. Interventionist, yes. Effective, also yes.

If we accept that 20 per cent of the steel industry, of the high street, of the nickel market, bestows too much power – forcing Canadian factories and Russian factories to close, wiping out the hopes of entire communities – then we must surely impose similar regulating structures and systems elsewhere. Make money. Enjoy. But we'd like to know what you're up to – and if you're going too far it's going to cost you.

Regulation refugees – the super-rich who dodge government regulation by moving their companies and themselves to stay ahead of tax rules and corporate rules – Cassidy believes, could be tamed by co-operation between relatively few governments: Tokyo, London, New York, Paris and Frankfurt could organize an equal, united system of regulation so that the money would struggle to evade, in the long run, and cost this would make sense. There are already signs of this in the co-ordination between London and Paris on limiting bankers' bonuses – limits created by popular demand.

That, of course, is up to us. We have to remind our leaders that we are the reason everyone's making so much money and wielding so much power.

We are at a critical point in history. The markets are weaker, more unsure than they have been or will be for years. And that makes the oligarchs vulnerable, too. But the stakes are high. If we fail to act, they will be stronger than ever before – there is no real attempt to construct a new deal or ensure improved social justice from the debris of the crash. And so we will all be left alone, each standing on our own tiny, barely farmable patch of polluted land in front of our tiny smallholding, outside a billionaire's factory, staring up at a monstrous, bleak and uncaring heap of polluted waste. We will all become Strike Matsepo.

REFERENCES

Unsourced quotes are derived from interviews conducted between October 2008 and November 2009.

Prologue
1. *Daily Telegraph*, 21 January 2007.
2. Martin Ravallion and Shaohua Chen, 'The Developing World is Poorer than We Thought', World Bank Development Research Group report, 26 August 2008.
3. Simon Johnson, 'The Quiet Coup', *Atlantic Monthly*, May 2009.
4. 'The State Strikes Back', *Sunday Times*, 29 May 2009.
5. Hansard, House of Lords, 13 November 2007.

Chapter 1
1. *Daily Telegraph*, 2 August 2008.
2. David Hoffman, *The Oligarchs: Wealth and Power in the New Russia* (New York, 2003), p. 360
3. Lev Timofeev, 'The Initial Theory of the Illicit Drug Industry', paper delivered at an international meeting of anti-prohibitionist drug reformers at the European Union headquarters in Brussels, 15–16 October 2002.
4. Chrystia Freeland, 'A Falling Tsar', *Financial Times*, 1 November 2003.
5. Ibid.

Chapter 2

1. *Sunday Times*, 22 February 2009.
2. *Sunday Times*, 20 July 2008.
3. *Sunday Times*, 12 October 2008.
4. *Financial Times*, 29 December 2008.
5. Richard Behar, 'Capitalism in a Cold Climate', *Fortune*, 12 June 2000.
6. *Observer*, 3 June 2007.
7. Judgment delivered at the Royal Courts of Justice, 3 July 2008, Case No. 2006, Folio 1218.
8. *Pravda*, 6 November 2009.

Chapter 3

1. *Hansard*, House of Commons, 5 March 2002.
2. *Evening Standard*, 11 September 2007.
3. *Irish Examiner,* 19 February 2002.

Chapter 4

1. www.Bhopal.org.
2. *The Times*, 5 September 2005.
3. Nitish K. Sengupta, *Inside the Steel Frame* (New Delhi, 1995), p. 62.
4. Hamish McDonald, *The Polyester Prince: The Rise of Dhirubhai Ambani* (Chicago, 1998), p. 66.
5. Ibid., p. 5.
6. Raham Rajan, 'Is There a Threat of Oligarchy in India?', speech on 12 September 2008; see: http://faculty.chicagobooth.edu/raghuram.rajan/research/papers/.

Chapter 5

1. Deng Xiaoping, excerpts from talks given in Wuchang, Shenzhen, Zhuhai and Shanghai, 18 January–21 February 1992; see http://www.olemiss.edu/courses/pol324/dengxp92.htm.
2. 'The Curse of Forbes', Forbes.com, 13 April 2009; 'Chinese Billionaire Home Appliance King Detained', Agence France-Presse, 24 November 2008.

3. 'Huang Guangyu, China's Richest Man, Disappears', *The Times*, 25 November 2008.
4. Deng Xiaoping, excerpts from talks given in Wuchang, Shenzhen, Zhuhai and Shanghai, 18 January–21 February 1992; see http://www.olemiss.edu/courses/pol324/dengxp92.htm.
5. 'Six Cities: China's New Aristocrat Consumption Threshold Report', *Hurun Report*, 29 July 2009.
6. 'China Weatherman Zhu Loses Grip', *Bloomberg*, 24 February 2008.
7. Aaron Solano, *Leadership Biography of Mr Reng Zhengfei, CEO Huawei Technologies Inc., China* (MIT, California, May 2007), p. 5.
8. Ibid, p. 2.
9. Evan S. Medeiros, Roger Cliff, Keith Crane, and James C. Mulvenon, *A New Direction for China's Defense Industry* (Santa Monica, CA, 2005), p. 218.
10. John J. Tkacik, Jr, 'Trojan Dragon, China's Cyber Threat', Backgrounder 2106 (Heritage Foundation, Washington DC, February 2008).
11. 'Spy Chiefs Fear Cyber Attack', *The Times*, 29 March 2009.
12. 'Chinese Investment Minefield', *Australian*, 16 December 2009.

Chapter 6
1. 'World's Economies Ranked by GDP', World Bank, October 2009.
2. World Bank Development Indicators 2008, see web.worldbank.org.
3. 'Rating Action: Moody's Upgrades Brazil to Baa3 and Assigns a Positive Outlook', Global Credit Research, Moody's Investor Services, 22 September 2009.
4. 2009 World Wealth Report, Capgemini and Merrill Lynch, 24 June 2009.
5. 'Strike Looms at Vale Inco's Sudbury Operations', Reuters, 11 July 2009.
6. Chris McGowan, 'Rio and the 2016 Olympics', *Huffington Post*, 2 October 2009.

7. 'Billionaire Batista Interested in Vale Stake', *Bloomberg*, 22 September 2009.
8. *Money Week*, 27 June 2008.

Chapter 7
1. Simon Johnson, 'The Quiet Coup', *Atlantic Monthly*, May 2009.
2. Ibid.
3. Matt Taibbi, 'The Great American Bubble Machine', *Rolling Stone*, 2 July 2009.
4. Joe Hagan, 'Tenacious G', *New York Magazine*, 26 July 2009.
5. Ibid. The account of the meeting is largely drawn from this article.
6. 'Eight Days', *New Yorker*, 13 September 2009.
7. Larry Elliott and Jill Treanor, 'Lehman Downfall Triggered by Mix-up between London and Washington', *Guardian*, 3 September 2009.
8. Joe Hagan, 'Tenacious G', *New York Magazine*, 26 July 2009.
9. Simon Johnson, 'The Quiet Coup', *Atlantic Monthly*, May 2009.
10. Michael Lewis, 'The Man Who Crashed the World', *Vanity Fair*, August 2009.
11. David Barrie, 'John Whitehead, Goldman Sachs and the New Commandments', 1 March 2001; http://davidbarrie.typepad.com/david_barrie/2007/03/this_is_john_c_.html.
12. 'How David Cameron is Trying to Buy the General Election', *Daily Mirror*, 26 November 2009.

Chapter 8
1. 'An Alternative Report on UK Banking Reform', Centre for Research on Socio-Cultural Change, University of Manchester, November 2009.
2. 'Private Equity in the UK in the First 25 Years', the British Private Equity and Venture Capital Association, April 2008.
3. *Daily Telegraph*, 21 June 2007.
4. *Financial Times*, 3 June 2007.
5. *Guardian*, 13 June 2007.
6. Sir Paul Myners, Letter: 'Private Dangers', *New Statesman*,

19 February 2007.

7. 'Party Finance Analysis Q2 2009', Electoral Commission, available at electoralcommission.org.

Chapter 9

1. *Guardian*, 4 March 2003.
2. *Sunday Telegraph*, 21 April 1991.
3. Alexandra Shulman, 'Throwaway Fashion', *Daily Mail*, 3 June 2006.
4. *Observer*, 18 June 2006.
5. *Daily Mail*, 21 May 2004.
6. *Independent*, 13 July 2006.
7. *Independent*, 5 July 2006.
8. Stewart Lansley and Andy Forrester, *Top Man: How Philip Green Built His High Street Empire*, p. 254 (London, 2005).
9. *Retail Week*, 16 July 2009.

Chapter 10

1. *The Times*, 25 November 2009.
2. 'An Alternative Report on UK Banking Reform', Centre for Research on Socio-Cultural Change, University of Manchester, November 2009.

FURTHER READING

Bouquet, Tim and Ousey, Byron, *Cold Steel: The Multibillion Dollar Battle for a Global Industry* (London, 2008)

Brainard, Lael and Martinez, Leonardo, *Brazil as an Economic Superpower* (New York, 2009)

Cassidy, John, *How Markets Fail: The Logic of Economic Calamities* (London, 2009)

Ellis, Charles, *The Partnership: The Making of Goldman Sachs* (London, 2009)

Frank, Robert, *Richistan* (New York, 2007)

Greenspan, Alan, *The Age of Turbulence: Adventures in a New World* (New York, 2008)

Hiscock, Geoff, *India's Global Wealth Club* (Singapore, 2008)

Hoffman, David, *The Oligarchs: Wealth and Power in the New Russia* (New York, 2003)

Hutton, Will, *The Writing on the Wall: China and the West in the 21st Century* (London, 2008)

Josephson, Matthew, *The Robber Barons*, (Orlando, 1962)

Lansley, Stewart and Forrester, Andy, *Top Man: How Philip Green Built His High Street Empire* (London 2005)

Lansley, Stewart and Hollingsworth, Mark, *Londongrad: From Russia with Cash* (London, 2009)

McDonald, Hamish, *The Polyester Prince: The Rise of Dhirubhai Ambani* (Chicago, 1998)

Midgley, Dominic and Hutchins, Chris, *Abramovich: The Billionaire From Nowhere* (London, 2004)

Rothkopf, David, *Superclass: The Global Power Elite and the World They are Making* (London, 2008)

Sengupta, Nitish K., *Inside the Steel Frame: Reminiscences and Reflections of a Former Civil Servant* (New Delhi, 1995)

Sixsmith, Martin, *The Litvinenko File* (London, 2007)